About the Author

Talbot Stevens is the president of a financial education firm that specializes in teaching people how to benefit financially *without sacrificing* their standard of living. Through his employer-sponsored and public workshops, you learn not only how to increase investment returns, but more importantly for many, how to lower costs and free up money to start investing.

With degrees in Engineering and Computer Science, he objectively identifies simple ways Canadians can be more effective consumers *and* investors. He has also started a petition to make basic financial education a part of the school system.

Talbot grew up on a small farm in Southwestern Ontario. He currently resides in London, Ontario, with his wife Theresa and their young, tireless, endurance testers, Derek, Ryan, and Kristin.

Financial Freedom Without Sacrifice

Financial Freedom Without Sacrifice

How to Cut Expenses, Invest and Increase Security Without Lowering Your Standard of Living

Talbot Stevens

Financial Success Strategies

Published in 1993 by
Financial Success Strategies Inc.
42 Fawn Court
London, Ontario, Canada
N5X 3X3

Twelfth Printing, July, 1999

Although every effort has been made to ensure the accuracy and completeness of the information contained in this book, the author and publishers assume no responsibility for errors, inaccuracies, omissions, or any inconsistency herein. Readers should use their own judgement and/or consult a financial expert for specific applications to their individual situations. Any slights of people or institutions are unintentional.

The story presented in this book is entirely fictional. The resemblance of any of the characters to actual persons, living or dead, is purely coincidental.

Significant volume discounts are available to purchase books to promote a product or service, or for fund-raising purposes. See inside back cover for details.

Canadian Cataloguing in Publication Data

Stevens, Talbot, 1965-
    Financial freedom without sacrifice : how to cut expenses, invest and increase security without lowering your standard of living

ISBN 0-9696873-0-3

1. Finance, Personal – Canada. 2. Financial security. I. Title

HG179.S84 1993   332.024'00971   C93-093571-3

Editor: Gilda Mekler
Cover Design: Barry & Weedmark Advertising & Design Inc.
Artwork Design: Sylvie Verwaayen

Printed in Canada

To Theresa, for her love, patience, and support

To my parents, for the *real*
education that everyone needs

To the millions of Canadians who, through no fault
of their own, are paying more than they need to, and
receiving lower investment returns than they deserve

GUARANTEE

To encourage everyone — especially those who have never considered buying a personal finance book — to benefit from these simple, untaught strategies, any Canadian between the ages of 20 and 55 is **guaranteed to achieve a Total Lifetime Benefit of at least $500.**

If, after reading the story and the *Quick Reference Strategies*, you feel that you cannot cut expenses and/or increase your investments by at least $500, either now or in the future, return the book in good condition, along with your receipt, to Financial Success Strategies for a full refund.

Contents

Part One: Journey to Financial Fitness

Part Two: Quick Reference Strategies

Free Up Money Without Sacrifice

Successful Investment Strategies

Preface

Most people know that there are more important things in life than money — but try to tell that to your banker when you're behind a couple of payments!

Now, more than ever, your financial success depends more on what you know than how hard you work. Ironically, in a world where we make dozens of financial decisions every week, we are not taught how to manage our money.

Fortunately, as you will discover in Part One, a fictional story, taking control of your financial future is easy. As illustrated by the story's financial illiterates in their journey through the hurdles of everyday finances, **anyone can achieve *Financial Freedom Without Sacrifice* simply by understanding a few basics and applying simple common sense**. By using an entertaining 'novel' approach to make learning fun, the process of cutting your expenses and increasing investment returns is made not only more appealing, but even enjoyable.

Part Two contains over 150 *Quick Reference Strategies*, together with real-life examples quantifying their benefit. It allows you to quickly identify which strategies you can benefit from, and doubles as an index.

It is important to realize that achieving your own financial freedom means much more than having enough money to do what you want, when you want. The real gains are the emotional benefits — the peace of mind that comes from the security of not having to worry about being laid off, losing the house, or whether you'll have a retirement fund large enough to enjoy the lifestyle you've looked forward to for decades. A healthy financial life often results in less stress, better relationships, and a happier, longer life in general.

As you are reading, be careful to resist the temptation to quickly skip over ideas that appear to be 'obvious' or 'common sense'. Unfortunately, common sense doesn't always translate into common practice. Take a close look at your own situation to ensure that you are benefiting from each strategy that applies to you now, and review the *Quick Reference Strategies* annually to identify new opportunities as your circumstances change.

To help future generations get the education needed to succeed in today's financial world, Financial Success Strategies has started a petition to make basic financial education a mandatory part of the school system. If you would like your children and grandchildren to benefit from this knowledge, you and/or your organization are invited to send signatures supporting this petition to the address below.

I wish you all the best, and trust that the ideas presented here will help turn your financial dreams into reality.

To your success,

Talbot Stevens
Financial Success Strategies Inc.
42 Fawn Court, London, ON N5X 3X3

Part One

Journey to Financial Fitness

◄ 1 ►
Life Is Great, Except . . .

Sometimes you wonder if you've made the right decision.

Not until my wife Theresa and I brought home the ultrasound picture of our baby-to-be did it really hit me. Now there was physical proof. I was going to be a Daddy!

Like any first-time parent, I tried to imagine what becoming a father would mean, and how it would change my life. After I asked our good friends Rob and Lisa Thompson how kids had affected their lifestyle, Lisa handed me a letter Rob had left her after an evening alone with their one-year-old son and black Labrador, Jake.

The water-stained note made me laugh — and wonder.

Hi Honey,

An Evening in the Thompson Household

Dog fussy – put outside for first time in four hours

Child fussy – put in tub for bath

Dad fussy – sits on toilet while bathing son

Child – always eager to explore his world, learns how to remove cap from shampoo

Dad – a prisoner of circumstance, watches helplessly as child empties shampoo in tub, creating world's largest bubble bath

Child – quick to take advantage of opportunity, has time of life covering self, walls, and floor with bubbles

Dog – now barking outside

Dad – finishes as quickly as possible (no easy task you know). Drains tub; rinses child, walls, tub; wipes floor.

Dog – stops yelping. Maybe he is contentedly playing. NOT!

Dad – gets child in towel. Goes to get 'dawg'. Opens door, but alas . . . It's not Jake, but CUJO (i.e. Jake after excavating back yard in the pouring rain)

CUJO – a.k.a. Jake a.k.a. 'dawg' bounds past Dad and still dripping son (who, by the way, thinks this is all hilarious) and races to top of stairs

'Dawg' is covered (I mean black dog is now brown) in mud. New carpeting on stairs, floor, and kitchen now mud.

Dad – puts dripping child down. Wrestles CUJO into basement. Covers self in mud. Are we having fun yet?!?

Attempt to put P.J.s on child. 'Dawg' yelping and child repeatedly screaming 'DAWG! DAWG! DAWG!'

Remind self that parenthood is a wonderful and sacred thing!

Child finally sleeps. Dad takes first breath in twenty minutes. Someone should tell Guinness!

Uncage and shampoo CUJO — Jake returns

Wash steps, landing, floor, and kitchen

Consider trading eighty-pound 'dawg' for small, quiet 'caat'

Pour large drink. Decide to keep 'dawg'.

Crawl into bed — but forget it's garbage night

Out of bed, into rain, take out garbage, crawl back to bed

> *So, how was your evening???*

Visualizing myself in Rob's shoes running after a wet one-year-old and a muddy dog, I asked myself, "Is this what being a father is all about?"

I was determined not to lose my excitement about having our first baby. I love kids and had been wanting one of our own ever since Theresa and I married. After all, what rational adult isn't eager to pay hundreds of thousands of dollars in return for something that cries all the time, keeps you awake at night, rarely listens, . . . and one day becomes a teenager?

As one of the two partners in this pregnancy, I think that I have definitely chosen to be the right one. When you add up all of the work (or is that labour?) that is involved, I think that if it were up to men to bear the offspring, we would all be only children. Even during the pregnancy, before the b-day (D-day for some), the man's role has certain advantages. For example, as a man, I can sleep through the entire night without having to get up three times to go to the bathroom. I don't get tired or nauseated, and I don't have to go out and buy clothes for someone twenty pounds heavier than I am.

With all of this said, Theresa is just as excited about having a baby as I am, possibly more so. Since the start of her pregnancy, she has been preparing for the baby as if it could come tomorrow. One of her plans, however, involves more than acquiring a crib and a change table.

We had talked about buying a house, and although it often seemed like an uphill battle, we had been saving for almost two years now. My plan was to move from our two-bedroom apartment into a house in two or three years, when we had a larger down payment.

Unfortunately, Theresa had been given a different script on how life should proceed. Her version said that you go to school, get a job, buy a house, and start a family — *in that order*. She reasoned that since the family was on the way, we had only a few months to buy a house. Having never ventured into the confusing world of mortgages, I was not in any hurry to commit to the responsibilities of a lifetime of mortgage payments.

Theresa was also concerned about my missing a prenatal class or two. It didn't upset me though, since that's how I went through school. Besides, what happens if you don't pass the course? Does the baby stay inside until it gets the signal from the course instructor that the parents are ready? I'm sure that none of this concerned my mother when she was having me and my three younger brothers.

Having grown up on a farm, it almost seemed appropriate for my parents to have four boys. Naturally, they were happy that we were to become parents ourselves. For my mom, Theresa's pregnancy was another chance for a girl in the family, something she had always wanted.

But there was more.

From my past, after a few of my episodes of less-than-perfect behaviour, I could hear my mom's vengeful wish echoing in the back of my mind, "Someday, I hope you get married and have kids just like you!" It seemed that she was also enjoying the fact that her day would soon come.

As I said, my mom was thrilled about the coming of the first grandchild for several reasons. She has been waiting for us to have a baby since our wedding, and has impatiently dropped hints and gifts ever since. Initially, she just asked in anticipation "Any news, Talbot?"

Then gifts started to bear a consistent message. Our first Christmas together, she gave us a very entertaining book entitled *Babies and Other Hazards of Sex*. It was signed 'With Love and Hope', with a double underline under 'Hope'. Then there were the ceramic dolls of a pregnant woman and her happy children. Finally, last Christmas, we received a rocking chair.

Another example of their direct and creative communication came on my eighteenth birthday. Instead of the normal sweater or shirt, my parents gave me a suitcase of my very own — and a map. On the map, someone had taken a black marker and drawn several large arrows — all pointing away from home! Loving parents, but not always very subtle.

But things had changed since I had left the small farm near Dresden six years ago. When I was young, the way to keep weeds out of the field was to send the kids out with hoes. Now, you simply spray a few times. During the fall, I used to pick and load tomatoes. Today, a $250,000 machine harvests the entire crop at once because the fruit has been genetically engineered to ripen at the same time.

Yes, times were changing, and more quickly than ever before.

That is probably why I left the farm to become a computer programmer. It's not that I didn't enjoy the sweaty, dirty, twelve-hour days, because I did. But everyone knows farmers are poor — just ask them, they'll tell you. And like most people, I didn't want to be poor. Being a billionaire wasn't necessary. But a nice home, regular vacations, and the ability to retire in comfort were definitely part of my plans.

So I decided to go on to college in London. For three years I studied and partied — not always in that order. In addition to picking up a diploma in Computer Science, I also met my wife.

Theresa was studying nursing at the University of Western Ontario. For some historical reason, nurses like to hang out with engineers. Through Theresa, I eventually got to know some of the more creative engineering students, the kind that felt a personal responsibility to keep life interesting. Because they, like me, were also concerned with school's opportunity for social and cultural development (partying and pranks), I fit right in.

One of their more entertaining stunts involved suspending a car fifteen feet up in the air, *around* a flag pole. From a distance, the car appeared to have been impaled by the forty-foot pole — no doubt the consequences of getting one-too-many parking tickets. Realizing that the car would not remain up the pole forever, the enterprising engineers had considerately fashioned an 'ACME QUICK RELEASE LEVER', clearly labelled for the authorities.

Those were the good old days, when responsibility meant making sure you got to the beer store before it closed.

After finishing her nursing degree, Theresa took a job with one of the local hospitals. I worked as a programmer, or computer analyst as we like to be called, for the Board of Education. Although Theresa's position as a nurse was fairly secure, mine was not.

These days, it seems that no one has job security. In my dad's era, a job with one of the mega-corporations like GM or IBM was considered a career for life. Now, even civil servants can lose their jobs with a budget cut.

As one of the newest programmers for the board, I was uncomfortably aware that my position would be one of the first to go if budgets dried up. With a family on the way, and a house purchase looming on the horizon, I couldn't afford to be unemployed.

But it was reassuring to know that Theresa, who finished near the top of her class, is smarter than I am. Not only does this increase our financial security by knowing that she could probably always have a job if she wanted one, our relationship is also much happier because of it.

For example, instinctively she seems to know not to rely on a man's memory for important things — like anniversaries and birthdays. Ever since the first time that I (almost) forgot her birthday, she has left multiple reminders on my calendar like, "Last chance to get your sweetie a gift."

This helps me, because it eliminates the need to lie and say that I remembered, but planned to take her out to dinner instead of buying a gift. (Note that this only works if she points out the birthday to you before dinner time.) More importantly to her, the timely reminders ensure that she gets a nice gift and the day isn't spent wondering why she married someone so insensitive.

Although I looked forward to the warmth and new life that summer brings, there was one aspect that I did not welcome. The sunny skies and lengthening days signalled the end of another hockey season for me and my buddies. Every Saturday night, we would take in a few shifts of hockey in an 'old-timers' league. In this league, anyone of legal drinking age is considered an old-timer, so we all qualified.

Afterwards, we would cool off at London's zaniest watering hole and restaurant, Joseph Koolisky's, commonly known as Joe Kool's — Kool's for short. Self-proclaimed as "undeniably the world's worst restaurant", the owner only assured that the food was better than at *some* hospitals. But what do you expect from a place where the menu includes TV dinners?

Here we told tales about our on-ice heroics while we watched the last part of the Leafs game. After a few beers, we would go home to our wives or girlfriends. All except Scott, of course.

As a bachelor, my best friend, Scott Martin, enjoyed the freedom of being single and had no intentions of converting. With his sparkling blue eyes and ready charm, he had no trouble meeting women. But marriage would take time away from his real passion — sports. Outside of his time spent working for a local auto parts manufacturer, if he wasn't actively playing a sport, he was watching one.

But Scott did love kids. Despite having no children of his own, every summer he coached a rookie baseball team and this year he had talked me into helping him.

With Scott around, I could stay active in the best way possible — playing. For me, other popular approaches to fitness didn't seem to work. I once tried joining a gym to lose some weight, but after twelve months, the only thing I had lost was the four hundred dollar membership fee.

For Scott, life was for living — each day another opportunity to have fun. Secretly, I had to admit there were times that I envied his carefree attitude. One day, on the spur of the moment, he joined some skydiving buddies and jumped out of an airplane because "it sounded like fun". He was also a regular traveller and rarely knew exactly where he was going until the day the plane was leaving. Instead of booking his trip in advance like normal people, he preferred last-minute seat sales — not to save money from the discount, but to add a sense of adventure.

With the baby expected sometime in November, Theresa and I decided to take our vacation early this year, and joined Scott and his girlfriend-of-the-month at a cottage up north. During our short but fun-filled seven days, we enjoyed all of our favourite water activities. By day, we were on the lake windsurfing and water-skiing until exhaustion. Then, to recuperate for the evening's festivities, we would practise our casting techniques, treat the hungry fish to a smorgasbord of expensive bait, and invariably end up catching nothing but some sleep and a few rays.

On our way back home from the cottage, I couldn't help feeling good about the few days up north, and life in general. From my perspective, life looked pretty good. I didn't need an extended stay in the Antarctic to make me appreciate just how fortunate we really were.

As a nation, Canadians enjoy one of the highest standards of living in the world. Within Canada, London was arguably one of the nicer cities, particularly for an ex-farmboy who didn't want the busier lifestyle of something bigger. The way I figured it, we were living in one of the best places on earth.

Yes, life was great. After years of financial struggle through college, it was good to be finally earning some money. With a loving wife and a child on the way, the future couldn't have looked brighter.

Little did I know that **something was about to transform our lives forever**.

⊰ 2 ⊱
I am Financially Illiterate!

"Do you know where we are?" Theresa demanded.

"Of course I do!" I lied, hoping my faked confidence would reassure her. "Just relax and enjoy the scenery."

Twenty minutes later, after we had made countless turns in the thick of Northern Ontario's wilderness, Theresa broke the peaceful silence again. "Isn't that the same house we passed half an hour ago?"

"Where?" I replied, now regretting my suggestion to observe the scenery.

"We've been travelling in circles! We're lost! You always do this when we go someplace new. Why don't you stop and ask someone for directions?"

"I don't need directions. I know exactly where I am," I defended. Theresa didn't understand that asking for directions is *admitting* that you're lost. And for a man, that is worse than being lost.

"And why do you have to get upset when someone decides to do a little unscheduled exploring? I thought you would enjoy seeing more of the beautiful countryside."

Yes, it was good to be married. Otherwise, how would I know when I was driving too fast or too close to the car in front of me? Despite Theresa's misinterpretation of my scenic touring, we were soon safely home in familiar surroundings where I was less likely to get lost.

Later that night, without any warning, it happened.

The phone rang and Theresa answered it. It was my mom. There had been a car accident, and Uncle Joe was dead.

I was not prepared for this. All of a sudden, one of the accidents that you hear about every day affected *my* life.

Uncle Joe, a few years younger than my dad, was too young to die. Although we hadn't seen much of him since he moved away fifteen years ago, he had been a big part of our lives when I was a kid. He was always fun to be around and told the best stories about his travels to exotic places like Africa and South America. With a Masters degree in geology, he was the scholar of the family and we had all looked up to him.

Then I thought of Aunt Shirley and her three teenagers. Without their husband or father, their lives would never be the same. As I grieved for Joe and his family, my impression of how good life seemed was now a distant memory.

A few weeks later, we learned that Shirley was selling her house. She said that she could no longer afford the mortgage payments and had to move into an apartment. With no career or education, she was concerned about how she would get by.

But how could this be? Certainly Uncle Joe had life insurance to protect his family in this situation. Why would Aunt Shirley be so concerned about finances? Needing to know, I picked up the phone.

"Dad, why is Aunt Shirley selling the house? Didn't Joe have life insurance to take care of things?"

"Yes, he had insurance," he replied, "But it wasn't much, only $25,000. Apparently, when Joe took it out twenty years ago, it seemed like plenty. But with inflation over the years, that doesn't go very far today.

"I guess that's why Shirley wants to sell the house. After paying for the funeral, there wasn't much of the insurance settlement left. With the mortgage and all of the other bills to pay, she doesn't have much choice."

"But they must have had other money or investments," I assumed.

"Besides a few thousand dollars in Canada Savings Bonds, most of their money was in their house. You know how much they liked to travel. And with one income and three teenagers, there wasn't that much extra money left over. You'll find that out soon enough."

"Yeah, I'm sure I will. Well, we'll probably see you on the weekend. Theresa says that she wants to help pick strawberries again before the end of the season."

"All right. We'll see you then."

I hung up the phone, bewildered. Why was Uncle Joe underinsured? He had always been so responsible. Yet, a few days later, I discovered something even more disturbing.

After one of our ball games, I was telling Scott how it surprised me that Joe had such a small life insurance policy. The father of one of the boys must have overheard us and joined the conversation.

"Excuse me, but did you say that your uncle died with only $25,000 of life insurance?" he asked.

"Yeah, why?"

"Well, that's unfortunate, especially since life insurance is so inexpensive," he said.

"What do you mean inexpensive?" I shot back. "I'm paying about $1,200 a year for $100,000 of insurance."

"You're kidding! It shouldn't cost that much for simple term insurance. How old was your uncle?"

"Forty-two."

"That's about how old I am, and I pay less than $600 a year for $300,000 of insurance. Your uncle probably could have had a similar plan."

"No," I corrected, "in hindsight, we can say that he *should* have had a similar plan, or even more coverage."

"I'm sorry, I didn't introduce myself. I'm Doug Parker, Billy's dad."

"Nice to meet you, Doug. I'm Talbot Stevens. Scott asked me to help him out with the team this year."

"It's good to see you out to lend a hand. The boys can certainly use all the help they can get. Well, I'm sorry to rush off, but I was supposed to pick up my wife ten minutes ago. We'll see you next week," Doug said as he headed off to his car.

★ ★ ★

That night I couldn't get to sleep. The conversation with Doug Parker had stuck in my mind. He had said something about simple term insurance. Although I hadn't thought about my life insurance since I bought it six years ago, I could still remember that it was anything but simple.

Even more intriguing was the statement that although he was probably fifteen years older than me, he had three times as much insurance, yet was paying half as much. At that moment I made a very simple, yet profound observation. Aside from what the insurance agent had told me, I knew absolutely nothing about life insurance.

Obviously Uncle Joe knew little more about insurance than I did, or he would have been properly insured. Unfortunately, his family was now paying for that ignorance.

I thought about Theresa wanting to buy a house later this year before the baby came. Despite the fact that the house would probably cost over a hundred thousand dollars, I also had to admit that I didn't know the first thing about mortgages or buying a house.

Soon I realized that I didn't know anything about taxes, investing, planning for retirement or anything that affected *our* financial success. I was financially illiterate!

But *why*? How is it possible for someone with a college diploma to know nothing about a subject as important as money? Did I skip so many classes that I totally missed the one on 'How to Insure Your Family' or the one on 'How to Invest and Retire Comfortably'? Nah. It would have been on the exams.

Anxiously needing a second opinion, I nudged Theresa beside me.

"Darling, wake up," I urged.

"Huh, what? What's wrong?"

"Did you ever take any courses in high school about insurance, mortgages, investing, or anything like that?"

"No, why?" She was still half asleep.

"In university?"

"No, nothing in university either, although I do remember learning about the importance of a good night's sleep. Can we talk about this in the morning? I really need some rest."

"All right. Go back to sleep."

Satisfied that I had found the root cause of my illiteracy, I became angry at our education system. Although we have one of the best school systems in the world, it's apparent that at least one subject has been overlooked.

What was the purpose of school if it wasn't to prepare you for survival in the real world, where you make dozens of financial decisions every month? Some decisions, like mortgages and life insurance, involve hundreds of thousands of dollars!

Then I thought about the difference a little insurance education would have made for Aunt Shirley. Why are we taught about amoebas, when someone with a Masters degree doesn't know how to protect his family's financial future?

Why don't we learn the answers to more practical questions, like: How do we insure ourselves properly at the lowest cost? How do we save and plan for an early retirement? Are there ways to reduce our mortgage costs? What is the best way to finance our children's education? How can we get out of debt and take control of our financial life? What can we do to reduce the incredible amount of tax we pay?

After acknowledging my financial illiteracy and seeing first-hand the consequences that can result from it, I promised myself that my financial ignorance would never harm those I cared about. From this point on, life would be different. I vowed to **approach every major financial decision only after acquiring some basic knowledge and applying simple common sense**.

Like most people, I generally did apply common sense. But Uncle Joe had common sense, lots of it. That was not enough. Without a basic understanding of all of the available options, no amount of common sense would enable you to choose the best one.

By committing to this simple two-step approach of understanding the basics and applying common sense, I already felt better about our financial future. I knew that Theresa would never become a widow forced to sell the house.

I decided to start learning about life insurance immediately. If what Doug Parker had said was true, we were spending hundreds of dollars a year unnecessarily. And money was already tight enough! I needed to find out **how to get more life insurance for a fraction of what I was already paying**.

◄ 3 ►

Save Thousands on Life Insurance

When Theresa walked into the kitchen the next morning, she noticed something odd about my shoes which were up on the counter.

"Talbot, why do your shoes look like they've been in the toaster?"

"Ah, . . . ," I said sheepishly. "It's a long story and I really don't want to go into it now."

"Tell me about it," she persisted. "I've got lots of time, I'm young."

"It all started with the coffee machine. I was — "

"You didn't forget to put the pot in the machine again, did you?"

"Yes."

"But the brown on the shoes doesn't look like a coffee stain." She was puzzled.

"No, it's not from the coffee that ran off the counter and onto the floor. When I got up, I remembered that I had washed my shoes yesterday and suddenly realized they were still wet. Since I didn't have much time before work to get the shoes dried, I needed to speed up the drying process."

"So?" she prodded.

"So, I stuck them in the microwave."

She shook her head and chuckled, no doubt reaffirming the benefits of not being dependent on a thick mug of coffee to jolt her into consciousness.

"You know, you can be dangerous before that first cup of coffee. You could have started a fire!" she scolded.

"I know. After a few seconds, I remembered that the metal eyelets for the laces could catch fire, so I quickly took them out.

14

"But I still needed my shoes dried, so I stuck them in the oven. I figured they would be safer in there because it is a nice, dry heat. . . . I guess I forgot about them while I was cleaning up the mess."

"You know, the guys at work are going to get a kick out of this when they see your shoes."

"Yeah, I know."

And they did.

It wasn't until that evening on the way home from work that Theresa remembered being awakened the night before. After I explained my unhappy discovery of being financially illiterate, she also had to admit that the system had failed to teach us the nuts and bolts of financial management.

"It's funny that we learned so many different things in school, but never once talked about managing our money. We're certainly not the first to realize that we're financially ignorant. I wonder why they still don't teach us about money in school," Theresa pondered.

"I don't know, but you'll be happy to know that I'm not going to let it affect our financial future. Blaming the system doesn't fix anything. And even if they made basic financial education a part of the school curriculum tomorrow, it wouldn't help us. We're out of school now.

"If we want to **avoid making financial mistakes** and **take advantage of financial opportunities** that we're not aware of, we need to learn a few basics. You can't expect to win the money game if you don't know the rules."

"So you're going to make sure that what happened to Aunt Shirley never happens to us?"

"That's right. I'm meeting one of the fathers from the baseball team right now. I don't know how, but he says I should be able to get more life insurance for much less than what we're paying now."

As I arrived at the Parkers' that night, I could see Billy and his dad playing baseball in the backyard. I approached Doug and suddenly the ball was coming at me.

"Talbot, catch!" Billy screamed.

"Good arm, Billy. You keep throwing like that and someday you'll be playing for the Blue Jays," I yelled back to the seven-year-old.

"Hello, Doug. It must be nice to have a son and a big backyard so you can throw a few balls around."

"It is. It's one of the reasons we bought this place. By the way, congratulations. Scott tells me you're going to have a ball player of your own soon," Doug said as the two kept playing.

"Thanks. My wife and I are pretty excited about it. I can't wait to be able to play catch with my own son or daughter," I said. "Anyway, the reason I dropped by was to talk a little about life insurance. You got my attention when you told me how much you were paying for your insurance. How can you get a better deal when you're older than I am?" I asked.

"I think I know why. I've seen it many times," he replied. "The policy that you have, is it a whole life or term insurance plan?"

"What do you mean?" I replied, revealing the depth of my financial knowledge.

"Do your premiums stay the same for the rest of your life and do you have something called a 'cash value'?"

"Yes," I answered, finally understanding the question.

"That's what I thought, and that's probably the biggest reason why your insurance is much more expensive than mine. Although I'm no insurance expert, I can tell you a few of the biggest and most common mistakes with life insurance. Avoiding them should save you a few hundred dollars a year."

"What are they?"

"Well, probably the biggest mistake is buying the wrong type of policy."

"The only types I'm aware of are complicated, and more complicated," I muttered.

"That's true," he agreed. "Most life insurance policies definitely are complicated, and for a reason. But the good news is that if you buy the right type of insurance, it is very simple to understand — even simpler than car insurance. Not only can everyone understand it, but it's also the cheapest and best value."

"So, what's the right type of insurance?"

"Most people should only buy simple term life insurance. Term insurance protects you for the length of the term: five years, twenty years, whatever you want. You simply pay the same premium during the length of the term and if you die, your dependents receive the face value of the policy, tax-free. It's even simpler than car insurance because there are no deductibles. If you're dead, which is easy enough to prove, the company pays. If you're not, you keep paying the premiums."

"You're right, that is easy to understand. But what about the whole life policies like mine?"

"According to my sister-in-law, an insurance agent herself, there are really only two basic types of life insurance: straight term life insurance and everything else. A term policy is pure insurance that anyone can understand. Everything else is a combination of insurance and a savings plan, and is so confusing that the average consumer can't hope to understand it.

"What you have is a whole life policy," he continued. "Sometimes it's called permanent or cash-value insurance. The problem with these plans is they are the most expensive protection you can get. Worse than the fact that you can end up paying five times more than you need to, the plans are so expensive that most people can't afford adequate coverage. The result is paying way too much for too little insurance."

"But what about the fact that the savings in a whole life policy can be used for retirement?" I objected skeptically.

"You've probably heard the expression '**Buy term and invest the difference**'," Doug assumed. "You'll always be further ahead to buy basic term insurance and invest the savings yourself. By keeping your insurance and investments separate, you will have more control and be able to get better returns on your own.

"The other reason to stay away from whole life policies is that — Hey, watch where you're throwing!" Doug was interrupted by one of Billy's throws that got away on him and nearly hit me in the leg. I decided it would be a good idea to pay more attention to the ball, particularly when it was coming towards me.

"As I was saying," Doug resumed, "the other reason to stay away from **whole life** policies is that **although you pay for both insurance and a savings plan**, you **cannot get both**. I'll bet you thought that if you died, you would get both the insurance and the savings."

"Of course."

"I'll also bet your agent didn't tell you that if you die, you only get the insurance payout, and the company keeps your cash value savings."

"No, he didn't." After a pause, I carried on. "I'm starting to see how easy it would be for someone like my uncle to end up with not enough of the wrong kind of insurance."

"For whole life policies, there are only two ways to get your cash value portion," Doug explained. "The first is to cash in your policy, which means cancelling it, leaving you without insurance. The other way is to borrow from your cash value, and amazingly enough, pay interest to use your own money! And if you do decide to borrow from your policy, your coverage is reduced by the amount that you borrow. How many banks do you know that charge you interest to borrow your own money?"

"None," I said. "That doesn't make sense."

"So you can't get the savings unless you reduce or eliminate your coverage," Doug resumed. "You obviously have to be alive to do this. But the only way to get the insurance portion of the policy, the face value, is to die! Since even Houdini would have a tough time being both alive and dead at the same time, it is impossible to get both the insurance and the savings."

"Even though they are sold as if you get both," I added.

"Unfortunately true," Doug confirmed.

"But the agent made it look like the cash value, after twenty or thirty years, was worth more than the premiums I paid. This made me think that I could get all my money back later if I wanted to. Isn't this a good idea?" I asked naively.

"Ah, the old 'add up the premiums' gimmick. Let me see if I can explain it like this. If you had put a dollar in a bank twenty years ago, how much would it be worth today?"

"I don't know, but it would be more than one dollar."

"Much more. And if you put a dollar in the bank every year for the last twenty years, wouldn't it be worth much more than twenty dollars?"

"I guess you're right."

"So, if that same bank — or the insurance company in this case — gave you back twenty dollars today, you really wouldn't have all of your money back, would you? That's because money does not have a constant value. Properly invested, money grows with time.

"But you don't have to worry about whole life insurance or trying to understand it. All you have to know to get the best value life insurance is two things. One: buy only simple term insurance. Two: **If you have a whole life plan, you could benefit three ways by switching to term insurance**.

"Depending on your age, your premiums could go down, while at the same time increasing your coverage. The third benefit is that you'll get your cash value out, which would have been kept by the company if you had died.

"The only practical way to get the cash value is to cash in the policy, *after* getting replacement term coverage. This sometimes frees up thousands of dollars, that can be used to start, or increase, your investment plan.

"That's about all I know," he concluded. "If you need life insurance, **only own simple term insurance**. If you do that, you'll get the best value and should be able to afford enough insurance to properly protect your family."

"Well, thanks a lot, Doug. I really appreciate it, and my wife will too. Do you think I could get the name of your sister-in-law? I'd like to give her a call and see what she can do for us."

"Sure. Her name is Maria Fernandez. You'll find her number in the phone book. She is one of the few life insurance agents that sells only term life insurance — what's best for the consumer," Doug replied, as he turned towards his son.

"Billy, that's enough for tonight. Go in and get ready for bed now," he instructed.

"Come here for a second, Billy. I've got to tell you something. You've got a strong arm. If you keep practising and work on your control a little, maybe we can get Scott to let you try pitching. Would you like that?" I offered, trying to encourage him.

"Yeah! That'd be swell! Can we practise again tomorrow night, Dad?" he shouted with excitement.

"Sure son, now let's get in and get ready for bed."

"Well, I'll let you go. Thanks again for the info Doug. We'll see you on Wednesday," I said, sincerely grateful for the advice.

After setting up a meeting with Doug's sister-in-law, I realized that I still had a few questions that needed answering. For starters, I still didn't know how much insurance would be enough. Seeing what happened to Aunt Shirley, I certainly didn't want to be underinsured.

But, at the same time I didn't want to be grossly over-insured either, because that would cost more money, taking away from my enjoyment of life now while I was alive. And overinsuring could also lead to a dangerous situation that many people don't consider.

All relationships have both good times and bad. If you make the mistake of having too much life insurance, it's possible that — during the heat of an argument — some spouses might add things up like this. Alive: you're a pain in the neck. Dead: you're worth one million dollars! The next day you're walking down a busy street with your spouse, and with a little help, you end up under a bus!

No, even though I know that Theresa would never do such a thing (I now make her walk streetside), I didn't want to overinsure either.

Remembering my school days, when I would occasionally discover useful information in books, I set off for the library. There I found a buyer's guide to life insurance — just what the doctor ordered. The book confirmed what Doug had said, and offered other useful tips on how to play the life insurance game and win.

When Maria Fernandez, the life insurance agent, arrived at our apartment the next evening, I was envious to see that she was carrying a laptop computer. Even though my career was in computers, I still didn't have one of my own. After introducing ourselves, the three of us sat where all formal business matters were discussed — the kitchen table.

"Maria, Doug tells me that you're the kind of agent that recommends only what's best for the customer, not what's best for you, the agent. Is that true?" I asked, really meaning to say 'Is that possible?'.

"Yes," she said frankly, "but don't take my word for it. You should judge for yourself after you hear my analysis and recommendations. But I have built a reputation for putting the client's interests first, for recommending the highest value insurance instead of selling the product that makes me the most money.

"After the first couple of years, my clients were so pleased to get low-cost, easy-to-understand insurance that they started referring their friends to me. Now, because I spend most of my time with clients instead of trying to find them, I am making more money and my conscience feels good about it.

"Now, the first thing I try to make my clients understand is the real reason to buy life insurance. In some cases, people don't need any at all. So tell me Talbot, why do you want life insurance?"

"Well, I want to make sure that if I die, Theresa will be able to raise the baby without having to worry about money," I replied.

"I didn't see a baby. Are you expecting?" Maria asked, looking at Theresa.

The ten-pounds-heavier-than-normal Theresa beamed back a smile of appreciation. "I like her!" she proclaimed. "I'm due in November."

"Well, congratulations! You definitely do have a need for insurance. The purpose of life insurance is to provide your dependents with necessary income that would be lost in the event of your death. Single people might want life insurance to cover their debts and funeral expenses, but the most important reason to have life insurance is to protect your dependents.

"The next question to answer is how much insurance to get. This is an area where many people really mess up and it either hurts their families or costs them extra."

"Yeah, I believe you," I interjected. "My uncle died recently, leaving little more than enough for the funeral."

"That's too bad. It really isn't difficult to determine how much insurance is needed," she asserted. "The thing that most people forget about is inflation. They buy some insurance when they start their family and never think about it again because it's supposed to protect them for their 'whole life'. As you probably know, with the inflation we have had over the last few decades, what may have seemed like plenty twenty years ago can barely buy a car today.

"Although it's really up to you to decide how well off you want your dependents to be should you die, I think that most people would want all their debts paid off and at least enough income to take care of the kids until they leave home. Some people may want enough life insurance to ensure that their dependents never have to work again, but I don't necessarily agree with that."

"I don't either," I said, remembering the bus. "I don't want to leave Theresa on easy street the day I die or she might start to look forward to it. Besides, as a nurse, she should never be in dire straits since she can make decent money even part-time, if necessary."

"That makes sense. Now, what debts do you have that should be covered?"

"Well, we both still have the student loans, and a few thousand on credit cards. The ten-year-old car has long been paid off. So, I would say about ten thousand," I said, thinking aloud.

"And what about the mortgage? You forgot about the mortgage," Theresa insisted, looking at me.

Up until this point, we had still not agreed on when we would get a house. After hesitating a moment, I added, "And the mortgage." Once again, Theresa was smiling contentedly. She now knew that she would have her own home for the baby.

"You'd better figure about another hundred thousand or so for a mortgage. We're going to be buying a house in a few months," I instructed.

"So, about a hundred and twenty thousand should cover immediate debts and funeral expenses," she concluded.

"Now, Theresa will also need money to live on. I generally recommend adding about five times your annual income. That way, if the money returns ten percent interest, she will end up with fifty percent of your current salary. With the mortgage paid off, most people won't end up lowering their standard of living at all.

"If Theresa has difficulty getting a good job, or inflation gets out of control, you might want to add more than five times your salary. Another approach to deal with inflation is to simply re-evaluate your insurance needs every three to five years," she explained. "I do that automatically, as a service to my clients."

"Since Theresa likes to work and is very employable, I think that five or six times my salary should be fine. If we need to add more later, because we have eight kids, we'll take care of that then," I said, noticing Theresa's eyes double in size at the thought. "So, add another $180,000 for income to the $120,000 to cover the debts to make an even $300,000 total. With that, and the small amount of insurance that I have through work, she should do fine."

"Good. Now, let's determine how much insurance Theresa should have," Maria pushed on.

I sat puzzled. I never thought about Theresa needing insurance. But now that I think about it, it would be just as difficult for me to raise a family on my own. More correctly, remembering my few failed attempts at managing the house on my own, and the fact that she currently makes more money than I do, it would be even tougher for me. But I couldn't admit that to them.

"I'm glad you brought that up. We should have $300,000 on Theresa as well."

Then Theresa spoke up. "What about the baby? Should we have a policy for the baby, or a plan to provide for its education, like my parents did for me?"

"No, it doesn't make sense to insure a baby," I said, demonstrating the benefits of having read up on life insurance. "How much money will the baby make, and who is financially dependent on its income?"

"No one, I guess."

"Precisely," Maria took over. "One of the **most common mistakes** people make, especially single people, **is buying insurance when they have no dependents**. The other advice that some agents give, which also isn't right, is that a cash value insurance policy is a good way to finance a child's education. That is one of the worst ways to achieve that objective, and is clearly a case of the agent putting their own interests ahead of the client's."

"I'm sure that's why my parents bought a policy for me. But when I got to university, the cash value was so small, I decided to keep the insurance," Theresa noted.

"I assume that neither of you smoke," Maria continued.

"No, we don't."

"That's good, because life insurance costs almost twice as much for smokers as for non-smokers. If you know someone who has quit smoking, you should tell them that they should be able to lower their premiums by getting non-smoker rates."

A few seconds after getting our ages, she turned the computer towards us. "Depending on the company, the annual premiums for $300,000 of traditional whole life insurance range from about $700 up to $1,200."

"Why are the premiums so low?" I inquired in confusion. "The $100,000 whole life plan that I currently have costs $1,200 a year. That's one-third of the protection you're quoting here. What gives?"

"What some agents try to do is structure the plan so that, instead of paying for your whole life policy the rest of your life, you pay for it in ten or twenty years. This increases the annual premium, which of course increases their commission. After the ten or twenty years are up, the policy is paid up and you can stop paying the premiums if you want. Or, you can continue paying and build up the cash value, which — "

"Which the company keeps if you die!" I denounced. "Isn't that like stealing the person's savings?"

"In a sense, it is. And that's another reason I don't sell whole life plans. But in reality, the cash surrender value isn't yours until you surrender — or cash in — your policy. I'm sure, though, that many people believe that their survivors will get both the insurance benefit and the cash value, since they're paying for both."

"I did!"

"Unfortunately, there are a few agents that don't disclose the entire truth about whole life plans and there's no excuse for it. But there are also agents, like me, who try to help their clients get the best value and understand what they've purchased. Now I'll show you the biggest reason why people should buy only simple term insurance," she said as she turned the computer again so we could see.

"This is how much it will cost you to get the same coverage with term insurance, which can be automatically renewed every ten years."

"That's hundreds less than what I'm now paying for one-third of the coverage!" I blurted out. "Getting this **term insurance** instead of my whole life policy **will save us $900 each year** *and* **I get three times as much insurance!**"

"You seem excited, Talbot," she said quietly.

"Of course! That's a lot of money, particularly for us when we're just starting a family."

"And buying a house," Theresa reminded.

"You realize that you won't save $900 every year for the rest of your life, just for the next ten years," Maria pointed out. "At the end of the ten-year term, the premiums go up."

"So we're only ahead $500 every year for the second ten-year term?" I asked, still as excited as if we had won a lottery. But I had good reason to be elated. In the next ten years alone, we were going to save $9,000 in life insurance premiums — gaining much more than most lottery winners.

"Right. These are the premiums at the end of each term. The premiums are guaranteed not to exceed those amounts," Maria indicated.

"But what about longer terms, like twenty years, or longer?" I asked. "Are these a good deal for the consumer?"

"Generally, you're better off with short terms for several reasons. Short terms always have the lowest initial premiums, no matter what your age. Secondly, many people will not need life insurance later, when term insurance gets more expensive. This is because they have enough other assets and fewer dependents. It doesn't make sense to overpay today in order to lower the future cost of something you may not even need later.

"No matter what term you choose though, make sure that the policy is both **automatically renewable and convertible**. The renewable clause means you can renew the policy for another term no matter what happens to your health, generally up to age seventy. A ten-year term policy wouldn't be much good to you if you developed a terminal disease and couldn't automatically renew. Most term policies are renewable, but you should make sure just to be safe.

"The convertible clause allows you to convert the term policy to a permanent policy. This would only be useful if you needed life insurance past age sixty-five, and couldn't qualify for longer term insurance."

A few seconds later, she revealed even lower premiums for the same coverage for Theresa.

"I already have a small $10,000 whole life policy that my parents started when I was a kid," Theresa announced. "Should we keep it?"

"You're not the only one in this situation," Maria began. "Many people have small whole life policies that were taken out decades ago. As you pointed out, if you keep the whole life plan, you're getting the worst possible value.

"The other consideration is the cash value. Remember that the only real way to get back your cash value is to cancel the policy," Maria reminded. "Fortunately, this often leaves you with enough money to pay for years of better value term insurance."

"Many people can save hundreds of dollars every year by **replacing their expensive whole or universal life**

policies with low-cost term insurance. By buying term insurance and investing the savings yourself, you'll do much better than these so-called alternatives. I know that it's difficult to acknowledge past mistakes, but we can't change history. We can only correct things to prevent them from continuing."

"So, we'll definitely cancel my policy and get the right amount of term insurance," Theresa concluded.

"Only cancel *after* you get a new policy in place," Maria cautioned. "You don't want to cancel a policy and then find out you can't be insured for health reasons."

"What is that waiver of premium option? Does that mean we have the option of not paying the premium?" Theresa asked hopefully, pointing to the screen.

"Nice try," Maria smiled to commend the attempt. "But no. Effectively, the premium waiver is insurance on insurance. With it, if you become disabled or ill for an extended period, the insurance company will pay your premium until you're able to work. Like most options, it's expensive, and I don't recommend it."

"Another thing you'll want to stay away from, no matter who you get your insurance from, is participating policies that pay you dividends. Participating policies work by charging a higher premium, and then giving *some* of it back to you in the form of a dividend. Would you be further ahead if, instead of charging three hundred dollars, I charged four hundred and paid you back a dividend of fifty? I think by now you've gotten the message to **keep your insurance and investments separate**," Maria reiterated.

"One final point. Since you'll be getting a mortgage, you'll discover that you can also get life insurance from your lender to cover the balance of the mortgage. Sometimes this can actually be a good deal — at the start.

"But be careful with this though, because the payout decreases as your mortgage declines. What might be a good value initially, might not be so good ten years later when your mortgage balance is much lower.

"Even if you had mortgage life insurance, that would only cover the one debt. You would still need another policy to cover other debts and provide income.

"Generally, you'll also find that it is cheaper to get one larger policy instead of several smaller ones. This is because you only have to pay administrative overhead on one policy, and because you get lower rates as the amount of coverage increases, sort of like a volume discount." Maria finished.

"It's also easier to keep track of," Theresa, who did most of the household filing, added. "All things being equal, the fewer the policies and accounts, the better."

At that point, I knew that Maria was genuinely more interested in serving our needs than her own. She actually mentioned a competitor's product. That could cost her a commission. After personally experiencing the quality of Maria's service, I realized that there was such a thing as a good life insurance agent!

As we completed the paperwork to replace our policies, I felt confident that we were getting the one thing that is even more important than the lowest price, and that is someone we could trust.

"Is there anything else we should know?" Theresa asked.

"No, that should just about do it," said Maria, packing up her computer.

"Oh, before you go. You wouldn't know a good financial planner, someone I could talk to about finances in general?" I asked. "If we can save almost a thousand dollars a year by learning a little about life insurance, maybe there are other ideas we can benefit from."

"Well, I know lots of people who should be able to help you," Maria replied. "Are you looking for someone active in the business, or do you want to just chat with someone informally? The best one to talk to is my dad's old advisor. After establishing a reputation for being one of the most competent financial planners in the area, she retired two years ago. She's probably forgotten more about managing and investing money than most experts ever know. Not only that, she loves to share her knowledge, particularly with those who are eager to learn."

"She sounds perfect."

"Her name is Susan Mitchell," Maria said. "If she's not away, you should be able to reach her at home. Since her early retirement, she's been doing a lot of travelling, enjoying some of the money she accumulated by acting on her own advice. Sue will tell you everything you need to achieve your financial goals. She'll also teach you the **shortcut to success**."

"What is the shortcut to success?" I begged, skeptical that there could be such a thing.

"I'd rather leave that for her," Maria responded. "Give her a call. She'll be glad to explain it to you, and more. Suffice it to say you're on the right track."

"Good enough," I said, realizing that it was getting late. "We'll give her a call."

"And I'll check back with you in a week or so. In the mean time, if you have any questions, call anytime," Maria said as she handed me her card, leaving me wondering what the ex-financial planner's shortcut to success could be.

◄ 4 ►

The Shortcut to Success
in Any Area

"Hi Scott, Rob. How's it goin'?" I asked, arriving at the golf course for another chance to humiliate myself. Golf was one of the few sports that I didn't seem to be able to figure out. It fascinated me that I could have absolute control of a 3,000-pound automobile travelling over sixty miles an hour, but couldn't control where a one-ounce golf ball went to save my life. Maybe that was what kept me coming back.

"Good, Talbot, but we'd be happier if we were on the third hole now. What kept you?" Rob demanded.

"You guys know I play my worst golf in the morning. Why couldn't we play this afternoon like I suggested?"

"Rob's got company coming after lunch," Scott explained.

I suppose it could be true. On the other hand, it wouldn't surprise me if the story were made up just to get me to play while I was still half asleep. They've done worse to me before.

"Rob, how's the job search going?" I asked. Two months ago, Rob was enjoying his job as a sales manager for one of the furniture store chains. Now, he was another helpless victim of corporate 'downsizing'.

"It's tough," he replied solemnly. "I've never been out of work before, and there's not a lot out there right now. It was hard enough trying to keep up with the bills before. Now I'm finding out what it's like trying to survive on unemployment insurance."

"I'm sure you'll find something soon," Scott encouraged.

"I know you will," I reassured with conviction. Although years older than Scott and I, Rob had the energy and determination of a teenager. That, combined with his

30

sales experience, should make him a valuable addition to many companies.

"I hope so," Rob said flatly. "Otherwise, we'll have to borrow money from the in-laws to make ends meet."

Remembering that we were on the golf course to get away from our daily concerns, I asked, "Rob, did you really write that note about taking care of Jeffrey and your dog Jake? It was hilarious."

"Yeah," Rob perked up. "And unfortunately, it's a true story. But don't let Scott see it or he'll never have kids."

"Don't worry. I don't need any more reasons not to get married," Scott reassured. "Just seeing what it's done to you two is enough!"

After nine or ten holes of discussing how much trouble Rob's kids could get into, Scott's latest toy purchase, and of course, the Blue Jays' chances of winning another World Series, I brought up a subject we had never talked about before.

"Hey, do you guys know much about life insurance?" I asked, watching Scott's tee-off shot cruise 250 yards straight down the fairway.

"What do you mean?"

"Well," I explained, "when my uncle died without enough life insurance, it made me realize that I didn't know the first thing about managing our money. So I decided to do something about it and learn a few basics. After a little reading and talking to a good insurance agent, I learned how to save $900 a year on my life insurance *and* triple the protection."

"Wow!" Rob exclaimed. "That's a lot of money, especially if you save that amount every year. To be honest with you, I don't even know how much the family is insured for. All I know is that it's all lumped into one payment that comes out of our account every month. It's not like you think about life insurance every day."

"That's for sure," Scott added. "I don't think I've thought about my policy since I started it eight years ago."

"Why do you have insurance?" I asked. "You don't have any dependents." As we watched my third tee-off attempt drift silently out of bounds, it became obvious that the only thing that could bail me out was my most powerful wood — my pencil.

"You don't have to have dependents to need life insurance," Scott claimed.

"Scott, how much do you pay for life insurance?" I asked.

"Not much, a little over forty dollars a month. Why?"

"How would you like an extra $500 this year, and next year, and the year after, . . . for doing nothing?"

"I'd love it. Who wouldn't? What are you getting at? Are you saying I don't need life insurance?"

"Unless you're living with someone we don't know about, who would benefit from the insurance payout when you died?"

"No one, I guess. My parents would get whatever estate is left . . . but they don't need the money. But it's not just insurance," he reasoned. "It's a universal life policy that is also building up a cash value. The agent showed me how quickly it would grow and I was impressed."

"As I said, I've done a little reading and talking to a life insurance agent, and learned a few things you might not be aware of.

"First of all, you have to realize that whenever you're dealing with a commissioned salesperson, there is a always a *potential* conflict of interest, meaning that their recommendation might be influenced by what makes them the most money. Naturally, you, the consumer, want the product with the best value — the best product for the lowest cost.

"Let's assume for a minute that, like many people, you don't know which product is the best value," I elaborated. "What if the best product for you results in a commission that is *one-fifth* that of another product that the agent's company wants him to sell? If the agent is not the Pope, but just a normal person with a family to feed, which one do you think he's going to try to sell you?"

"I'm betting it's the one that makes the agent and his company the most money," Rob claimed.

"But at the time, my policy looked like a good investment," Scott argued, still rationalizing his decision. "The agent showed me how the cash value would grow over the years at ten percent. Isn't that a good return?"

"With today's interest rates, that might seem attractive. But if your policy was like mine, you'll find the returns aren't guaranteed, they're only *projections*. That means they aren't worth the paper they're printed on. Besides, only part of the premium goes towards the investment. The insurance book said that a big chunk goes to pay for the insurance, the agent's commission, and administrative overhead. The money spent on these things you never get back.

"Universal life policies," I went on, "are much better than the traditional whole life plans. You probably don't have as bad a deal as I had. As with my old whole life policy, your investment portion grows tax-free. More importantly, your dependents *do* get both the death benefit and the investment if you die. But most people would be better off to keep their investments and insurance separate — assuming, of course, they need both.

"Since the agent's commission alone can be as much as the first year's premium, many of these cash value plans have no savings value at all for the first few years. And it's not always easy to cash in the 'investment' — the fine print sometimes limits what you can do and there may be large penalties to discourage you."

"Let me get this straight," Scott said. "You're saying that by using a better investment, I could have more money working for me. And this is because the insurance, commissions, and policy overhead eat up much of my premium."

"Exactly."

"Well, I think I'll check it out. If what you said is true, and I do save a few hundred a year, I'll pay for the next nine holes," Scott promised.

"That would be a nice switch," I reflected, glad that my new financial knowledge was really starting to pay off. As an incentive to improve our golf, the loser had to buy the winner a beer. Now on the fourteenth hole, Scott was once again almost certain not to be buying. Rob and I were equally poor players, and break out the champagne whenever we break one hundred. And on the second nine, we usually do worse!

"So how did you save so much on your life insurance?" Rob wanted to know.

"It's actually very simple — once you know how," I declared. "The most important thing is to buy the right kind of life insurance. Term insurance can be as much as ten times cheaper than whole life insurance."

"But doesn't term insurance keep getting more expensive each time you renew, making it really more costly in the long run?" countered Rob, as he surprised us all by dropping a twenty-foot putt.

"Yes, term insurance naturally gets more expensive as you get older," I responded. "But that doesn't mean that it's more expensive over your lifetime. Term insurance is very inexpensive until about age fifty. Not long after that, you probably won't need life insurance any more, unless . . ."

"Unless what?"

"Unless you want to ensure that you have a certain size estate to pass on. People who own a business or a lot of real estate might want to have permanent life insurance like term-to-100 or a good universal plan to make sure there is enough of an estate to cover the capital gains taxes that must be paid at death."

"So you save almost a thousand a year just by getting the right life insurance?" Rob asked, impressed with how easily the benefits were achieved.

"Yep. That's it," I replied. "And if you're like me, you'll get back some cash value from the old policy that will put you even further ahead."

"Hey, could I get the name of that agent?" Rob inquired. "I should find out if we can save some money on insurance. We could sure use the extra cash these days."

"Her name is Maria Fernandez. She only sells simple term insurance and seemed to put our interests ahead of her own. She'll also explain how you can save money by not insuring your kids. Like Scott, your kids don't have anyone who is dependent on their income, so they don't need to be insured."

"Thanks, Talbot. I'll check it out. And if I save a few hundred dollars, maybe I'll buy you a round of golf too!"

"It'd be nice to have someone else buy for a change. It looks like I'm buying again," I said, as we finished our round and headed for the all-important nineteenth hole. "Rob, do you have time to join us?"

"No, I'd better catch you later. I've got to pick up some things before I get back."

With my debt to Scott still owing, the two of us returned to my place where Theresa was preparing a barbecue. Theresa's best friend, Kim Reynolds, was also there.

"Hi, Kim. Where's Rachel?" I asked, referring to her three-year-old daughter.

"I left her with a friend."

"How was the game?" Theresa inquired.

"It was good — beautiful day, lots of sun, good exer—"

"Who won?" Theresa impatiently cut off my attempt to avoid discussing the outcome.

"He lost," Scott announced as he retreated to the balcony to enjoy his thirst-quenching trophy. "Does she always look like that?" he whispered, nodding towards Kim.

"She's always looked fine to me," I replied, "especially in the summertime."

A tall brunette, Kim was very attractive, and frequently spoiled herself with new clothes. She hadn't dated seriously since her divorce, although it wasn't for lack of men trying. It still surprised me that Scott hadn't asked her out. He was obviously interested, at least from a distance. Perhaps he feared that if he got to know her better, he would not be able to resist her and would become one of us.

"Theresa, did you tell Kim about the good news?" I asked.

"What good news?"

"How we're saving almost a thousand dollars a year."

"No, tell me," said Kim. "If it's something I can do too, don't keep it a secret."

"Kim, would you be upset if you found out that a friend knew of a simple way to save hundreds of dollars a year — and they didn't tell you?" I asked.

"Of course," was her answer.

It's true that people don't want ideas forced on them, but when there is a large obvious benefit, I figure you owe it to those you care about to at least make them aware.

We learned that Kim was distressingly underinsured with a whole life policy, which could have left her daughter Rachel in a terrible situation. As a busy single parent handling all of the responsibilities of raising a child, she admitted she didn't understand insurance or most financial matters. In fact, when it came to money, she claimed to be good at only one thing — spending it.

Enticed by the idea of having more money available while responsibly protecting her daughter, Kim also promised to call our agent to improve her life insurance protection.

★★★

It took several attempts on different days before I finally got through to Susan Mitchell, the retired financial planner. She had just enough time for a brief meeting before she headed off on a trip through Europe.

We met at a doughnut shop the next night. I instantly liked Sue. She reminded me of my late grandmother when she was in her fifties. She was always happy; her ever-alert eyes beaming with childlike energy. Sue's genuine smiles and obvious love for life were contagious and forced you to smile right back. After knowing her for only a few minutes, I could sense that, like my grandmother, Sue's years of experience would be a source of both knowledge and entertainment.

"What would you like to drink?" I asked, standing at the counter to order.

"Just a coffee is fine. Black."

"I really appreciate you meeting me like this. I wanted to talk to someone who could teach me a few things about money in general. I don't need investment advice right now because I don't have any money to invest. Do you mind me asking how you became financially successful?" I inquired.

"No, I don't mind. We can talk about whatever you want," Sue said. After reflecting for a moment, she resumed, "Without a doubt, the biggest reason for my success is something I learned when I was even younger than you are. It's the most important thing I have learned in my entire life. I call it the *shortcut to success.* With it, you can succeed at anything in the shortest amount of time, with the least amount of money. Few people are aware of it because it's not something that's taught in school."

"I don't want to talk about what they don't teach in school. It only frustrates me. If school had taught me about money, we wouldn't — "

"Did you see that? A triple play! You don't see many of those," Sue burst out, pointing to the lone television in the corner of the cafe. "I'm sorry, go on."

"You were telling me about the shortcut to success," I reminded her.

"Yes. Have you ever used a recipe or a map? Of course you have. Everyone has. But *why?* Because if you want to bake a good cake, the easiest way to do it is to follow a successful person's recipe. By simply doing what the expert does, you can achieve the same results, often the first time you try.

"Everyone knows to use a recipe to cook. But what they don't realize is that just as there are expert cooks, there are experts in practically every field. If you want to improve your golf game, what do you do?"

"I obviously don't know. My game is consistently bad," I answered honestly.

"You study how the best golfers play and take lessons. You talk to them and try to find out how they do better than others. That is the **shortcut to success** in any area. Simply **study successful people and do what they do**. In other words, **model success**. With the proper role models, you can do in minutes what took them years to figure out.

"You would never try to drive to an unfamiliar place without using a map. Without taking advantage of the mapmaker's knowledge of what roads to take, the trip could take forever. And if you got lost, you would ask for directions, right?" she asked.

"Of course," I replied, thankful that Theresa wasn't there to contradict me.

"But most people don't apply that same principle to other areas of their lives. They want to be more successful in their careers, businesses, or their finances. But they try to do it without a map, without knowing what direction to take.

"In this information age," she continued, "**what you know is much more important than how hard you work**. The best thing about knowledge is that the benefits are so easily communicated. In the old days, the only way to make a dollar was to put in time and work for it. Today, knowledge that took experts years to learn is available in books, magazines, newspapers, on tapes, radio, television, everywhere. In minutes, you can benefit from their experience and use it as a shortcut to achieve whatever goal you're seeking."

"So you became wealthy by learning from other wealthy people and doing what they do?" I asked.

"That's part of it. I also learned a lot about being a good financial planner from my boss, who introduced me to modelling success. Not only did I learn a lot about money, but I also earned a decent income as well. It's not hard to make money — if you know how," she grinned.

"Well, that's what I'm here for, to learn how to manage our money better. After learning a little about life insurance, I saved $900 a year, and tripled my coverage!" I declared proudly. "I figured that since I essentially know nothing about most financial matters, there must be other areas I could also improve."

"You're probably right," she agreed. "What I learned about money over the years is one of the biggest reasons for what I have today. Let me make one final point. Why do people go to doctors, lawyers, mechanics, and other specialists? Do you think it's because their wallets get too thick and they can't wait to give their money to someone who charges a hundred dollars an hour? No, it's because they have no choice.

"But when it comes to finances, people normally don't seek professional help until they're either really rich, or more often, deep in debt or bankrupt. That's too bad, because with a little professional help, it's easy for most people to acquire more than they've ever dreamed possible.

"Unless you are a financial expert, there are dozens of ways to dramatically improve your financial situation, no matter what your goals are. **Everyone needs a good financial advisor** to help them with their money matters, the same way they need doctors or mechanics to deal with their health or car problems," Sue summarized.

"So, what are some of the ways we can better manage our money?" I asked.

"You say you saved some money on life insurance, eh?" she said. "Let me guess, you originally had a whole life plan and then discovered you could get more insurance for less money by buying term insurance. Is that about right?"

"Basically."

"And you saved $900 a year by switching?"

"And ended up with more insurance," I clarified.

"I know you're excited about the savings, but you actually gained much more than $900 a year."

"What do you mean?"

"Let's say you earn a dollar at work. How much of it do you get to take home, after taxes and other deductions?"

"I have no idea," I admitted. "All I know is that it never seems like enough."

"If you're in the middle tax bracket like most people, you get to take home less than sixty cents after paying income taxes. Then there are other deductions like pension plan contributions, unemployment insurance premiums, and benefits, so you only end up with about half of what you make, or fifty cents on the dollar. When you buy something, like insurance, you pay for it with money that has already been taxed — in other words *after-tax dollars*.

"So how many dollars do you have to earn to buy something that costs one dollar?" she asked, testing my understanding.

"Two. I have to earn two dollars to buy something that costs one," I replied, now aware that half of everything we earned went to the government.

"Now let's look at it from a different angle. Instead of spending a dollar, let's say you found a way to save a dollar. How much would you have to earn to end up with the same extra dollar in your pocket?"

"Two dollars. I just told you."

"Be patient," Sue warned. "It's very important that you understand this. So, a dollar saved is the same as . . . ?"

"Two dollars earned."

"Now you know that Ben Franklin's old saying that 'a penny saved is a penny earned', isn't really true in a country where you pay taxes. **A dollar saved is *two* dollars earned**," she summarized.

"So you're saying that saving $900 is the same as earning an extra $1,800?" I asked, finally realizing the importance of her point.

"Yes. You've given yourself an $1,800 a year raise! And how long did it take you?"

"A couple of hours."

"Now you're starting to see how valuable a little knowledge can be. Just remember that there's a big difference between *before-tax* dollars and *after-tax* dollars. Even though Canada is one of the most highly-taxed countries in the world, most people aren't aware of how taxes affect our decisions, both as consumers and as investors.

"Well, that's about all the time I've got for tonight," she said, glancing at her watch as she finished her coffee. "But before I go, I will point out that **most people can earn over twenty-five percent interest guaranteed**."

"How?"

"I don't have time to explain it tonight. I'm going to leave that with you to find out."

"Can't you give me a hint or something?" I pleaded.

"You've got everything you need. You've already started modelling success looking for shortcuts. You've been reading books and you came here to see what I could teach you."

"When will you be back from your trip? What if I don't figure out how to earn twenty-five percent interest guaranteed?" I blurted out.

"Don't worry. I'm sure you'll figure it out," she said, turning to leave. At the door, she looked back with a grin. "I'll be back in early January. If you haven't figured it out by then, you can always take me out for another coffee and I'll tell you!"

⊲ 5 ⊳

Save Hundreds on Car
and Home Insurance

Naturally, I was very curious and anxious to find out how to earn twenty-five percent interest guaranteed. I wished Sue had had time to explain how. If she hadn't already left the country, I would have called her to find out.

The bank had no idea. The best investments they offered paid less than ten percent interest. When I was in the bank, I noticed that you could get a personal loan for about ten percent.

That led me to a great idea. If we borrowed money at ten percent and earned twenty-five percent guaranteed, we would make a guaranteed fifteen percent, using no money of our own! The only problem was, how do we make twenty-five percent?

Remembering what Sue had said about the shortcut to success, I started calling financial planners. Several said that there were investments that *could* gain twenty-five percent in a year — but not guaranteed. They explained that the only way to achieve higher returns was to take larger risks. I translated this to mean that we could just as easily lose twenty-five percent as gain it. Why would we risk losing money to get higher returns when there was a way to get a great return guaranteed?

It puzzled me that the experts could not provide the answer. Their advice centred around suggestions like "pay yourself first" and "contribute to an RRSP". After explaining that we didn't have money to invest since everything we could save was going towards a house, I asked if they knew of other ways we could save money, like we had with life insurance. I also pointed out that we had no interest in setting up a budget to dictate how our money would be spent.

However, the financial planners only seemed able to help once you had extra money to invest. This was unfortunate, I thought. If they could show us how to free up money for investing, they would not only get our business, but also two happy clients.

My search for the elusive way to earn twenty-five percent interest was interrupted by a bill that arrived in the mail. Our car insurance premium was due.

Remembering how much the life insurance premiums varied, I decided to call a few insurance brokers to see if we could get a better rate. When I first took out the insurance, I had simply gone to my parents' agent, figuring what was good enough for them was good enough for me.

It surprised me to discover that the yellow pages listed what seemed like hundreds of companies looking for my business. After a few minutes on the phone, I had quotes from three different brokers, one higher than what we were paying, and two lower. The best quote was $250 a year less than our current premium! Although I realized that purchase decisions should never be based on price alone, I felt that several hundred dollars a year was too much to pay for any possible difference in service from our current agent.

It amazed me that fifteen minutes of **shopping around for car insurance could save us $250 a year**. That works out to a thousand dollars an hour for the first year's benefits alone! Geez, at this rate, we would be millionaires in a few months. Well, . . . maybe not, but I did recently receive this personal letter from Ed McMahon . . .

By getting the same product for less, we saved money *without* giving up anything. And because saving one dollar is the same as earning two, we were actually gaining $500 a year. At that point, I decided to **make shopping around for all major purchases a habit for life**.

Then I remembered Maria Fernandez, the agent who had been so helpful with our life insurance. She also sold general insurance so I called her.

"Maria, our car insurance is up for renewal and I was wondering if I could get a quote."

"Sure," she said. "We just need to know a little about you and the car."

With the details about the car and our driving records, she continued. "You want collision and comprehensive coverage?"

"Yes."

"And what size deductibles?"

"What do you mean?" I asked.

"The deductible is the amount you pay on any claim you —"

"I know what the deductible is," I interrupted. "I didn't know I had a choice of what it could be. All the brokers I talked to quoted a $250 deductible for collision and a fifty dollar deductible for comprehensive."

"Your deductibles have a big impact on what your premiums will be," Maria advised. "The lower the deductible, the higher your premiums are."

"So **if we increase our deductibles, we can lower our insurance costs**?"

"Exactly. Most people won't make a small claim anyway, because they don't want their rates to go up. If you're not going to file small claims, why have a small deductible?"

"What deductibles are available and what do you have?" I asked.

"Collision deductibles can be increased to $500 or $1,000," she went on. "Comprehensive deductibles can be increased to $100 or $250. By increasing my collision deductible to $1,000, and my comprehensive deductible to $250, I lowered my premiums by fifteen percent, saving over $100 a year.

"The higher collision deductible gives me more incentive to drive safely, since an accident will cost me more money, and I am rewarded with lower premiums. With a lower deductible you are penalized with higher premiums no matter how well you drive. And having the standard fifty dollar comprehensive deductible is really having no deductible at all, since most windshield and auto body shops will cover your fifty dollar deductible just to get your business.

"No one can afford to protect against every risk. That's why any insurance should only be used to protect against major losses — those you can't afford to handle yourself."

"How much would we save by increasing our deductibles to $1,000 and $250?"

"Just a second," Maria said as she checked the figures. "A hundred and four dollars," was the response. "People with poor driving records would save much more, and increasing their deductibles may be the only way to afford the premiums."

Everything Maria had said made sense. I'd been driving more than twelve years and had filed only one minor comprehensive claim. If someone had told me these things back in high school, our down payment for the house would be at least a thousand dollars larger.

"Are there other ways we can reduce our car insurance costs?" I wondered.

"Well, the biggest way to save is by shopping around. Some companies' rates can easily be thirty percent higher than others. You're doing that. If you qualify, there are certain discounts that can also reduce your premiums. You can get an abstainer discount if you don't drink," she added.

"I'm not willing to qualify for that!" I quickly pointed out.

"Did you take a driver's education course?"

"Yeah, back in high school."

"Well, that will save you a little. Oh, one more thing. Many people could save a couple hundred dollars a year by **dropping their collision and comprehensive protection when their vehicle loses most of its value**. It doesn't make sense to spend an extra three hundred a year to protect a $1,500 car, especially when you have to pay a deductible first."

Not only was that something that applied to us, it reminded me that we were thinking about getting a new car. Since I was soon to be a family man, safety was now more important than saving money by driving a car that doubled in value every time the tank was filled.

"Our car can't be worth $1,500. If we can go with a $1,000 collision deductible, we might as well drop the coverage completely," I stated, knowing that insurance companies rarely pay out what the car is really worth. "How much would we save by dropping collision and comprehensive and just getting one million in liability coverage?"

"Just a sec." Again, Maria checked some figures and replied, "Two hundred and thirty dollars."

"That sounds even better," I said. "Is there anything else I should know to lower our premiums?"

"Well, I don't think that we can sneak you in for a senior citizen's discount," she kidded. "But you will probably want to pay monthly, even if you can afford to pay the year's premiums in one shot."

"Why's that?"

"Because not only is it easier on cash flow, but in Ontario right now, the maximum interest rate that can be charged for financing your car insurance premiums monthly is three percent. Most people can invest their money and get more than that."

"While we're on the topic of insurance, what should I know about home or tenant insurance to make sure that we're not paying more than we have to?" I asked. "We have a tenant policy now, but as you know, we're getting a house soon."

"Aside from shopping around, of course, you can **save** fifteen to twenty-five percent **on your home insurance premiums by increasing the standard $200 deductible to $500 or more**," she said. "As with car insurance, low deductibles don't make sense and are very expensive.

"You should also get a discount on your premiums if you have a newer home, a security system, or get both your car and home insurance from the same company.

"The only other thing I can think of is to make sure you don't insure for more than you own. You don't want to insure your home for the price you paid, because some of the cost is for the land, which cannot be destroyed. You only need to insure the buildings and the contents. The same thing applies if you have a tenant policy. You're wasting money to have a $40,000 policy when you only have $10,000 of valuables. You can't collect more than you can prove you owned. That's why it's a good idea to keep photographs or a videotape of your valuables in a safety deposit box, or at work — anywhere but in the same house, just in case of a fire."

"Well, thanks a lot, Maria. Once again, you've shown me how to save some money. By the way, your approach of doing what's best for the customer is paying off. I gave your name to a friend of mine."

"You mean Rob Thompson. I appreciate the referral. We already met. You understand that because each client's affairs are strictly confidential, I can't give you any details — except perhaps that he said something about paying for your next round of golf."

"That's good. I'm glad you could help him," I said, thinking of how he needed the money, and more importantly, the free round of golf.

★ ★ ★

With July offering fresh strawberries, raspberries, cherries, and blueberries all ready at once, Theresa and I returned to my parents' farm to visit and enjoy nature's candy. Although it didn't bother Theresa much, we missed the annual highlight of the summer at the farm, the *Rutabaga Festival.*

For those who don't know, the rutabaga is one massive, yellow, beet-like root that can extend as much as a foot into the ground. Harvesting these stubborn things by hand is not a task for the uninitiated. In an effort to share the joys of the harvest, the event was coined the Rutabaga Festival. The name carried with it an allure of fun in the sun, and succeeded in attracting one or two friends each year to find out what the festivities were all about.

Dad had always said that hard work never killed anybody, but some people obviously didn't think it did them any good either. In all of the years the Rutabaga Festival has existed, I believe only one person was man enough to return a second time — and she was a woman. I doubt that she did it for the enjoyment or the challenge, but nonetheless, she proved she had something few others had — so I married her.

While Mom and Theresa were inside discussing preparations for the baby, I found Dad outside splitting wood.

"How come you're still splitting wood at this time of year?" I teased. "When I was home, all the wood was split and piled by early June."

"That's not true," he claimed, "and even so, we cut a lot less then. And this winter was so wet and mild that we couldn't haul wood out of the bush until spring."

My teasing didn't do me a lot of good. Immediately, he thrust an axe in my hands, as if to say 'stop talking and do something about it'.

"Dad, why didn't we ever talk about money?" I asked, changing the subject.

"What's there to talk about? You know that no matter what you want, there's only one way to get it — you have to work for it," he replied. "Money doesn't grow on trees, you know — unless, of course, it's an apple tree, and you sell the apples."

"Well, that's not totally true. Sure, you taught us to save for something we needed, and not to borrow. But there's more to managing your money than that. If Uncle Joe had the right amount of life insurance, Shirley wouldn't have to be selling her house now."

"That could be. But at least Joe had a will. Without a will, your estate could be tied up by the courts for years and could end up going to the wrong people. You do have a will, don't you?" he asked.

"No, I never even thought about it."

"Well, you need one. **Everyone needs a will** to ensure that their assets go to who they want, without unnecessary expense and delay. Although you can get a do-it-yourself will at a stationery store for a few dollars, I suggest you go to a lawyer and get one drawn up properly. They'll explain everything you need, and it shouldn't cost you much more than a hundred dollars."

"But why aren't we taught these things?" I wondered out loud. "Times have changed from hundreds of years ago when survival depended on how well you could grow and store food. Today, financial success depends not only on how well you can earn money, but also on how well you keep it. But if we don't know anything about money, and the bankers, insurance companies, and other businesses do, what chance do we have?"

"I guess for most people, how to handle your money is something you either pick up on your own, or you don't learn at all," Dad concluded.

"Saving money using a little know-how is certainly easier than working for it," I noted, feeling the raw of a good-sized blister, after only a few minutes of work. "So, I trust you've got enough life insurance to take care of things if anything should happen."

"Of course. But just in case, you've still got that spare bedroom, don't you?" Dad kidded.

By the time we were ready to head back to London, I had had enough exercise to last me a week, and Theresa had enough fresh berries to last almost as long. About halfway back to the city, something happened to the car that you would never want to happen when it's dark, raining, and you're away from home. With my foot still pressing the accelerator, the car started to slow down.

"Not the transmission!" I prayed, as I pumped the gas pedal. After rolling to a stop, I just stared at the pouring rain beating on the hood.

"Great! Now what do we do?" asked Theresa.

Not eager to exchange the dry shelter of the car for a brisk walk to the nearest farmhouse, I desperately searched for options. I tried reverse and was relieved to learn that we still had at least one gear. I shifted back into drive and . . . nothing.

Then Theresa noticed the '1' and '2' beside the 'D' on the steering column and remembered that automatic transmissions had first and second gears that you could shift into manually. I tried our last hope, and breathed a sigh of relief as we moved forward. Although we had lost the automatic drive, we still had manual first and second gears and were able to make it home.

The next day, it didn't take the mechanic long to conclude that the transmission needed major surgery. Based on the value of the car, he wisely advised us to let it 'rust in peace'.

With the impending financial expense, it was good to have learned how to cut our insurance expenses by over a thousand dollars a year. We were going to need the extra money — and more. I *wanted* to buy a computer, and we *needed* a new car. Talk about apples and oranges (or should that be lemons?). The only thing the two had in common was they both crashed a lot!

◄ 6 ►

Save Thousands
on Your Next Car

The timing of the car's breakdown couldn't have been worse. For months I had been talking about getting my own computer. I knew that if I was going to do well as a programmer, I had to do more than read books and magazines.

With every available penny already going towards the down payment, it made it that much more difficult for Theresa to understand spending a couple thousand dollars on a box that for her meant nothing but frustration and the occasional outburst of colourful language. Now that we needed a new car, it seemed all but certain that the computer purchase would be delayed indefinitely. I suggested to Theresa that she postpone the birth instead, but to no avail.

Having already decided that our first family vehicle was going to be a minivan, we set out early Saturday morning to see what the local dealers had to offer. I don't know why, but whenever we drove into a dealer's lot, salespeople seemed to race each other to get to us. I suppose it was possible, especially for a car salesperson, to take one look at our rusted, ten-year-old Chevy as it limped onto the lot and conclude that we *needed* a car. True, the car was definitely showing its age and was more than ready to be put out to pasture. Even with a new transmission, there was only one way that a mechanic could look at it and pass it for a safety — if he looked the other way.

As I had never seriously explored a dealer's showroom, my initial reaction to some of the prices was shock. The numbers on some of the luxury cars belonged on houses — not on five seats suspended on four wheels! Although the salespeople were very helpful in most ways, there was one thing that almost no one was willing to do.

"What's the *real* price of the van?" I demanded. "I see the MSRP, the Manufacturer's Suggested Retail Price, but you're not going to suggest we pay *that*?"

Like a politician, most answered the question with another question. "What can you afford?" or "Why don't you give me a price and we'll work from there?" After one sales rep dodged the question three or four times, I became so infuriated that I wanted to strangle him. However, I resisted the temptation, as I remembered that in some provinces, it is still a misdemeanor to kill a car salesman.

After several weekends of shopping around, Theresa and I decided on a vehicle that had everything we wanted. It even had a few options we didn't want, but the sales rep said that's the way the options were packaged. Just before going down to the dealer to sign the papers, I got a phone call that changed everything. It was Rob.

"Hi, Talbot, I'm just calling to make sure you know that hockey is starting in two weeks."

"Yeah, I know. Scott already told me. Thanks anyway."

"Oh, I called that insurance agent you told me about and I've got good news. Your next round of golf's on me!"

"I take it you saved a buck or two?" I asked smugly.

"Not exactly — $1,200 a year!" Rob exclaimed excitedly. "That's not even the best part. Before, we didn't even have enough insurance to cover our debts. Now, we're insured properly, *and* we have an extra hundred dollars a month to help us get by!"

In all the years I've known Rob, this was the first time I'd ever heard him talk about his finances with enthusiasm. Even before he lost his job, he was constantly half-joking about being in debt up to his eyeballs. Although he didn't show that it bothered him, perhaps joking about it was his way of dealing with a hidden stress.

"Fantastic," I said, glad Maria could help. "Rob, did I tell you we're buying a new minivan?"

"No. When are you getting it?"

"We're going down to sign the papers today."

"Hey, before you do, how much do you know about buying cars?"

"Not much," I grimaced.

"Well, maybe I can save you some money. I know this guy who used to sell cars. After he told me some of the ways dealers make most of their money, we ended up saving $7,000 on our last car."

"Well, what did this guy tell you? With the house and baby on the way, you're not the only one who needs all the money they can get."

"For starters," Rob proceeded, "you shouldn't let the dealer know that you have a trade-in until after you've agreed on a price. Announcing the trade-in at the start just complicates things and gives the dealer another opportunity to play with the numbers to work out in their favour."

"It's a little late for that this time. I was glad to get anything for it."

"You know that because the dealer has to mark up the price before they sell it, you can generally get more by selling your old car yourself, rather than trading it in," he reasoned. "Of course, you know to negotiate as hard as possible, by getting different dealers to compete against each other."

"We did shop around to compare, but I had a heck of a time trying to get the real selling price out of anybody. How do you know how much to offer, and when you've got a good deal?" I asked.

"You can **generally figure on negotiating down five to fifteen percent off the list price** — more for larger cars with lots of options, less for smaller cars. I'm sure you've heard that dealers make most of their profit on the options. Well, there are some options that are almost worthless, yet can cost you hundreds of dollars each. One of the worst options to buy is the rustproofing warranty."

"What's wrong with that?" I asked. "It seemed to make sense to me. After all, the body is one of the first things to go."

"That may be so. But most of these warranties are 'rust-through' warranties, where the dealer is only liable for major body work if a hole has rusted clean through. In other words, you have to be able to put your finger through it. You know that even the older cars took five to ten years before a hole would rust right through. By then, you probably won't even own the car."

I didn't have to be told that rust takes a long time to make a hole. Our ten-year-old Chevy had plenty of rust, but only one or two small holes.

"This guy also pointed out a couple of other options that you might want," Rob continued, "but not at the dealer's inflated prices. Fabric protection and paint sealant do make sense, but not for the hundreds of dollars charged for them. Twenty bucks worth of fabric protectant and regular waxing will do the same thing."

"I didn't even really pay attention to how much those options cost," I admitted. "I just knew that we wanted them. I guess when you're buying a car, you have to be careful every step of the way."

"No kidding," Rob agreed, "especially once you've decided to buy. But think about it a second. If the extended warranties and options were better for you than the dealer, do you really think they would try so hard to sell them to you?"

"No, I guess not."

"Hmm, . . . what else did he say?" Rob asked himself, trying to remember. "Oh yeah, don't fall for their low-rate financing tricks."

"You mean where they lure you into their lot, promising an unbelievably low interest rate? Then, after you've decided to buy, you find out that you only get the discount financing if you don't take the cash back rebate."

"Yeah, that's part of it. You either get a lower rate on a higher price, or a higher interest rate and a lower price. Compare these two alternatives with taking the cash back and getting the financing somewhere else, like a bank or trust company. The best of these three financing possibilities is the one with the lowest payment.

"Oh, that reminds me," Rob continued. "My friend suggested that you **finance the loan over two or three years, not four**. Apparently shortening the payback period saves you hundreds of dollars in interest, but doesn't really increase your payments much."

"Well, that's good to know," I said, grabbing a pencil to make a few notes.

"Another thing to **stay away from**," Rob went on, "is the **life and disability insurance** they'll try to sell you. Whether you get financing from the dealer or a bank, they'll try to sell you this insurance because it's another overpriced option."

"I didn't know that. But I don't think I would have fallen for that one, since I'm already properly insured."

"But the **best way to lower the cost of a car**," Rob said, "is not to buy a new car at all, but to **buy slightly used**, or one of the dealer's demonstration vehicles — the ones they use for test drives. The price of a demo can be ten to twenty percent less than a new one and they often only have a few thousand kilometres on them."

"We thought about buying used," I countered, "but we wanted a safe, reliable car that wouldn't give us a lot of problems. We didn't want to end up with someone else's troubles."

"Initially, I thought the same thing," Rob confessed. "I figured it was worth it to pay a little extra to buy brand-new. But by getting a car that *looks* like new, but doesn't cost like new, you can save a lot of money and still have the original warranty to cover you in case you've bought a lemon. Everybody knows that you lose thousands of dollars the minute you drive a new car off the dealer's lot. That's why you save so much by buying a demo. It's been off the lot a few times and can't be sold for the price of a new one."

"Is that what you did, buy a demo?" I asked.

"No. I bought from a guy selling his car privately in the newspaper. The price was such a steal that I thought there must be something wrong with it. But after getting a mechanic to check the vehicle over, it turned out that what the guy told me was true. With his wife just laid off, they couldn't afford payments on two cars and needed the cash."

"So you haven't had any problems with it?"

"Nope, and I've still got six months on the original warranty. Back when I got it, buying the same car new would have cost over $7,000 more."

"Wow! We might have to rethink this idea of buying new," I reflected. "If we could save that much money, we could . . ."

"You could what?"

"We could do a lot of things with seven grand," I replied, thinking of the computer, the house, the credit cards, student loans, . . . "Is there anything else I should know?"

"Yeah, I almost forgot. If you do buy a vehicle privately, make sure you get your banker to check that there aren't any liens against it."

"What's a lien?"

"That's when someone has the legal right to repossess the car, like when there is an outstanding loan or an unpaid repair bill. You certainly don't want to buy a car and then find out that you've inherited someone else's bills in the process."

"Good point. Is that everything?"

"Yeah, I think that's it. I hope that helps," Rob said, seeming to want to return the favour for the life insurance tips.

"It'll help a lot. Thanks a million. We'll let you know how we make out," I said. "Talk to you later."

When we returned to the dealer, I decided to check out some of the points Rob had mentioned. We still hadn't decided against buying new and wanted to evaluate the options more carefully.

With a few questions and a closer examination of the breakdown of the car's costs, we learned that the $500 rustproofing warranty was practically worthless. The fabric protection and paint sealant unnecessarily added another $300 to the bill.

Reluctantly, the sales agent showed us some of their 'previously owned' minivans. He was even more disappointed when I told him that we wouldn't be buying that day. I still wanted to check out some private sales and see what financing rate we could get from other lenders.

The weekend newspaper revealed three good possibilities for minivans less than two years old. After we viewed them, the one we liked the best happened to be the exact same model that we almost bought from the dealer. It was barely a year old and didn't have a scratch on it. After a few minutes of haggling with the owner, we settled on a price $6,000 lower than what we were going to pay for a new one! And with two years of warranty remaining, we didn't have to worry about major repairs.

Theresa was even more pleased than I was. "I've never bought used before," she mused. "But look at it this way. If someone offered to pay you $6,000 to drive your new car for a year, plus they covered all expenses like gas, maintenance, and insurance, would you take the offer?"

I thought about it for a moment. I remembered that we were borrowing the money, and with interest on the $6,000, the real cost would be closer to $8,000. Then I remembered what Sue had taught me about after-tax dollars — that saving one dollar is the same as earning two. This meant that saving $8,000 was the same as getting an extra $16,000 of income.

Would I accept a $16,000 bonus to let someone I didn't know drive our new car for a year? In a minute! I had never thought about buying a one-year-old car this way before, but it made sense. From now on, we were going to buy slightly used and upgrade more often, if we wanted to. After all, with the $16,000 bonus, we could now afford it! Besides, this way we could get a safe, newer minivan *and* a computer for less than we were originally going to pay for just the vehicle.

As we stood back admiring our biggest purchase ever, we had to admit that you couldn't tell the difference between a one-year-old vehicle and a new one — except for the price, of course. Reflecting on the common knowledge that cars depreciate about thirty percent in the first year, we concluded that it only makes sense to let someone else pick up the first year's depreciation tab.

With some of the savings, I bought my own computer. I tried buying used because there's only one thing that depreciates faster than a car, and that's a computer. But I wanted a faster, Oldsmobile-powered machine and most of the used computers for sale were beat-up Chevettes. So I had to buy new.

Now only four months from Theresa's due date, we shifted our priority to something more important than transportation or computers — a permanent roof over our heads. We already had a pre-approved mortgage from our bank to give us an idea of what price range we could afford.

In between outings with our agent to look at houses, I started reading a book about mortgages and playing with some loan formulas on the computer. Since the house would undoubtedly be the largest purchase of our lives, I wanted to make sure that we understood all of the basics before selling our souls to a banker to take on such a commitment.

Early in the book, I was shocked to learn that a normal $100,000 mortgage ends up costing an *additional* $210,000 in interest over twenty-five years. Then the book identified a simple way to cut the total mortgage interest cost by about a third! Relieved and grateful that I had learned this before taking out our first mortgage, I wondered if Rob, who already had one, was taking advantage of this effortless way to save tens of thousands of dollars.

◄ 7 ►
Cut Mortgage Costs
30 to 50 Percent

With Theresa a little under the weather for a couple of days, I had to pick up her share of the household chores. Unfortunately, this meant delving into some tasks that I not only lacked experience in, but was downright unqualified for.

Thanks to my mom, I was quite competent at everyday things like cooking and light cleaning, but for one reason or another, I had never learned to do laundry — at least not properly. This first, and hopefully last, time I did laundry, I threw all of Theresa's clothes, including her new purple dress, in the same load. When I discovered the results of my effort, I decided not to delay the inevitable, and to confess immediately.

"Darling, I've got good news and bad news."

Theresa, who was starting to feel better, asked for the worst first. "What's the bad news?"

"I dyed some of your jeans purple."

"Great!" she replied in sarcastic disappointment. "I just got those jeans. Can't I trust you to do anything?" She wasn't pleased. "What's the good news?"

"You now have some shirts to match!" As she complained about my lack of domestic knowledge and explained how it should have been done, I was glad I hadn't done any of my clothes. I hate purple!

Realizing that she couldn't afford to be off her feet long with me in charge, Theresa was soon feeling well enough to allow me to go with Scott to Toronto to see a Jays game. It was exciting to see the Blue Jays in the Sky-Dome as they headed into the stretch for the pennant.

"The Jays are going all the way this year," Scott forecast with confidence. Of course, he had predicted the same thing the last four years as well. "They've got solid pitching, and have been hitting great lately. They're definitely the team to beat."

"Well, we'll see," I said. "Hey, I hear through the grapevine that you're seeing Kim."

"No, we're not *seeing* each other. We just went out once or twice, the same way I've gone out with lots of other women." Scott's defensive tone told me that Kim was now more than his best friend's wife's best friend.

"All right, we'll see. You know I think there are worse women to get hooked up with."

"Nobody's gettin' married! We just went out a couple times. It's nothing serious." Scott's reaction confirmed my suspicion, and I didn't push the issue further.

"So how did you make out with your life insurance?" I asked, knowing that Scott would welcome a change of subject.

"Oh yeah, thanks. I owe you nine holes of golf. I checked into the universal life plan that was supposedly such a good investment. It was an expensive lesson, but the bottom line is that by cancelling, I save almost $500 a year on something I never should have had in the first place.

"But lately, I've been thinking about bigger financial matters," he went on. "With mortgage rates low, and housing prices soft, the rent I'm paying for my luxury apartment is almost as much as the mortgage payment on a good starter home."

"Since Theresa and I are getting a house, I've been doing some reading on the subject and talking to people," I explained, "and in most cases, buying a home is a great investment. I know that some people consider buying a home a quick way to get under a mountain of debt, but the right way to look at a **mortgage is as a leveraged, forced savings plan** into what has historically been one of the best investments — real estate. You not only get to enjoy living in it and the long-term benefits of ownership, any increase in value of your principal residence is tax-free when you sell."

"I know that real estate is a good investment in the long run, but what do you mean by a *leveraged* forced savings plan?" asked Scott.

"In investing, leverage is simply using a little bit of your own money and a lot of someone else's. If you buy a house with a ten percent down payment, obviously you borrowed most of the money from somebody else. But the valuable thing that leverage does is magnify your investment returns."

"How?"

"Well, let's say you buy a $100,000 house with a down payment of ten percent, or $10,000. If the value of the house goes up only five percent a year, which is about half of the annual gains that many areas experienced in the eighties, how much would the house be worth at the end of one year?"

"Add five percent or $5,000. So the house is worth $105,000."

"Right, the house increased in value by $5,000. But you only invested $10,000. You gained $5,000 on an investment of $10,000 in one year," I said. "That's an annual return of fifty percent! By using somebody else's money, you increased your annual return from five to fifty percent! That's what I mean by leverage."

Scott pondered what I'd said. "That's impressive. I could handle turning a five percent return into a fifty percent return. But housing prices can go down too, especially over the short term, as many people have found out. You also didn't factor in the extra cost of making the mortgage payments. Bankers don't like it when you don't make your payments, you know."

"Of course you have to make your mortgage payments," I replied. "That's why a mortgage is a forced savings plan. Once you start, you're forced to keep making the payments or you could lose the house. That's a pretty good incentive to keep up to date.

"But your return *is* almost fifty percent, even after accounting for the fact that you will pay thousands every year in mortgage payments. You see, your mortgage payment, like your rent, covers the cost of putting a roof over your head. It's a necessary expense. It doesn't matter whether you pay rent or pay a mortgage, you still have to pay for shelter."

"I don't believe it!" Scott shouted.

"You don't believe you have to pay for shelter?" I asked, confused how anyone could argue that.

"No, I can't believe that Cito isn't changing pitchers! Guzman doesn't have it tonight. He just walked the second batter in a row."

"Don't count him out yet," I warned. "He can still get out of the inning without giving up a run. I've seen him get out of tougher spots than this." There was reason for concern, however. With two on and one out, the Jays' three-run lead was threatened.

"I understand what you mean about having to pay for shelter whether you rent or have a mortgage," Scott continued. "That's why I'm considering buying a home. I figure if I buy now, I can probably get a place for about the same amount that I'm now giving to someone else. What kind of house are you and Theresa looking for?"

"Just a nice three-bedroom starter house in a nice neighbourhood, hopefully something that's close to a park, schools, and a bus route. The only thing I'm fussy about is getting a house that doesn't need a lot of work. I know you can make money in your spare time by buying the worst house on the block and fixing it up, but that's not the way I want to spend my free time."

"I wouldn't mind getting a place that needed a little work," Scott said. "That would help keep the cost down, and I could increase the value of the property at my leisure."

"Look," I shouted, referring to the double play that got Guzman out of the inning without allowing a run. "I told you not to count Guzman out too soon."

"I guess Cito was right," Scott admitted. "Sometimes you've got to have faith in your players and let them do their job. I guess that's why he's coaching the Jays, and I'm coaching Little League. So, how did you learn all this stuff about mortgages?"

"I started by talking to our real estate agent and then to a mortgage broker. The broker not only helped us by shopping around for the best mortgage, but also made sure we understood the basic definitions and options available. She also gave us an information package and told us about a free booklet for first-time home buyers.

"Then I picked up a book on how to cut mortgage costs and started playing with some mortgage formulas on my computer. That's when things got interesting."

"What do you mean?"

"Well, I learned a couple of simple ways to save tens of thousands of dollars in interest costs. Even better than that, I think I've found a way to cut the total interest in half *without* lowering our standard of living. I have to double check a few numbers, but I should be able to tell you about it Saturday after hockey."

"That sounds great — almost as good as the Jays' win," Scott said, as Toronto won their fourth game in a row. "Maybe affording a house will be easier than I thought."

"By the way, I think I found a goalie for Saturday nights. This new, self-employed consultant at work, Pierre Girard, says he can play," I informed Scott of the good news. Lacking a steady goalie meant we often had to take turns in net with a set of outdated equipment.

That Saturday night, hockey was no different than any other first outing of the season. Initially, most of the guys were really excited about getting back out on the ice to pop a few goals and occasionally greet a buddy with a friendly body check. But a summer of low activity had caught up to many of us 'old timers'. It took only a couple of laps around the ice to be rudely reacquainted with leg muscles that hadn't been used since last season. Only twenty minutes into our one-hour scrimmage, we were glad to get a rest on the bench and looked forward to more relaxing activities at Kool's afterwards.

When we finally arrived at the bar to lick our wounds, I introduced Pierre to Phil, the bartender. "Pierre, this is Phil. As long as you're not in a hurry to get a drink and don't expect it to be cold, Phil's the best beer slinger in town."

"That's right. What can I get you boys?"

"The usual for everyone."

"What'll you have, Pierre?" Phil asked.

"Give me a cold Blue."

"Pierre, you were awesome tonight," Scott complimented. I was equally impressed with how Pierre's
quickness and agility more than made up for his short,
thin stature. "You've obviously played goal before. You
think you can make it out every week? It sure would be
nice to have two goalies."

"Yeah, I'd like that," he replied. "After my divorce last
year, I've been trying to keep busy and get out of the
house more."

"Sorry to hear about the divorce," Scott said. "I have to
warn you though, if you hang around these guys long
enough, they'll probably try to get you hitched up again.
It seems they just can't stand to see a guy happy!"

"Thanks for the warning," came Pierre's grateful reply,
as he surveyed Kool's uniquely decorated interior. "Just
curious, but is the owner here a Tigers nut or something?"

Glancing at all of the baseball paraphernalia, including
the dozens of Detroit Tigers T-shirts and banners stapled
to the walls and ceiling, Rob answered, "He sure is —
poor guy. But I doubt he would be offended if you called
him a nut. He'd probably take it as a compliment!"

"Rob, I meant to thank you earlier for your tips on buying a car," I tossed in, breaking the laughter. "By buying
a one-year-old minivan, we ended up saving $6,000, more
than enough to buy the computer I'd been wanting for a
long time."

"That's good. So what'd you get?"

"A Ford Aerostar. Looks like new and has only 15,000
kilometres on it."

"And you finally got that computer you've been talking
about for so long?"

"Yep."

"We bought a computer for the kids last year, and to be
honest with you, I'm lucky if I can figure out how to turn
the thing on," Rob confessed. "All this talk about bits and
bytes . . . it just sounds like a high-tech snack food to
me."

"They're not that hard to use," I claimed. "The software
has gotten a lot easier to use in the last few years. I even

found a personal finance program that I've been using to learn about ways to reduce mortgage costs."

"Did you get a chance to check the numbers you needed?" Scott asked. "You said you found a way to cut your mortgage costs in half without lowering your standard of living."

"Yeah, I did. But before I explain it, I should make sure you understand some terminology. Scott, do you know what the amortization period is?"

"Isn't that the length of time it takes you to totally repay the loan?"

"Yeah," I acknowledged. "The normal amortization period for a mortgage is twenty-five years — most of your working life. It's important to distinguish the amortization period from the mortgage term, which is typically one to five years. At the end of the term, the mortgage contract expires, at which time you can pay off or pay down your mortgage without penalty, or you can renew it for another term."

"And that's when your payments can go up or down, depending on which way interest rates have moved," Rob pointed out.

Pierre jumped into the conversation. "Hey, do you guys know that you don't have to pay the mortgage renewal fee?"

"What do you mean you don't have to pay it?" asked Rob. "Don't bankers normally get upset when you don't pay your bills?"

"Not in this case. With the mortgage market so competitive, your lender will do almost anything to keep your business. I've even seen times when some lenders will pay you cash, in addition to covering any administration fees, to get you to switch your mortgage over to them."

"So I guess it pays to shop around, not just initially when you take out the mortgage, but also at each renewal," I affirmed. "That makes sense. I saved a couple hundred dollars by shopping around for our car insurance when it came due. A mortgage shouldn't be any different, and there's a lot more money at stake."

"I'll have to check out what the different lenders have to offer," Rob noted. "Our mortgage is up for renewal in a few months."

"Well, at the very least, you should save the eighty- to one-hundred-dollar renewal fee; that's almost a year's ice fees for hockey." Pierre seemed to be quoting from experience.

"Or a couple of nice dinners on the town," Rob said, rephrasing the benefit in terms he was more interested in.

"I thought you were going to explain how to cut interest costs in half — without sacrifice," Scott reminded me impatiently.

"Yeah, I *need* to know," Rob added. "I've *got* a mortgage. Scott doesn't even have one yet."

"I'm getting to that," I reassured them. "I just want to touch on some points that Pierre reminded me of before I forget. First of all, it's foolish not to shop around hard for the biggest expense of your life. Not just the house, but the mortgage. There are mortgage brokers who can shop around for you. Realize also that if your local bank doesn't initially appear to have the best deal, they will generally match the competition to keep the business.

"Using my computer, I figured out that just a **half-a-percent difference on a $100,000 mortgage can save you over thirty-five dollars a month**. That's $2,000 dollars over a five-year term.

"When you're comparing mortgages, there are a couple of clauses you should pay special attention to. If you get a long term, like five years or more, pay attention to what the early repayment penalty would be to refinance or pay off your mortgage before the end of the term. Our broker said the penalty is either three months' interest or something called an 'interest rate differential'. That's a fancy term for all of the interest the lender would lose by allowing you to refinance at the lower rate. Although most lenders charge the greater of the two penalties, some just charge three months' interest, which can be thousands of dollars less than the interest rate differential penalty."

"So a mortgage that has an early prepayment penalty of three months' interest is better?"

"Yes. You may never use it, but if rates drop and you want to refinance, this one clause can save you thousands."

"What about portability and assumability clauses?" Rob asked. "Aren't they important?"

"Sure, they're important." I replied. "The portability clause allows you to transfer your mortgage terms to a different house if you move. And it's equally important to be able to let someone else assume your existing mortgage if you want to sell."

"But those things don't lower your interest costs," Scott pressed again.

"True," I said, finally ready to address his concern. "The easiest way to lower your mortgage interest cost by about a third is simply to pay weekly or every two weeks, instead of monthly."

"That's it?" Pierre was disappointed. "Everyone knows that."

"I didn't know that," Scott admitted.

"I didn't either," added Rob. "And I've been making mortgage payments for almost ten years. How does that reduce your interest costs?"

"There's really nothing magical about it — once you understand what is happening," I claimed. "By paying half of your normal monthly payment every two weeks, you end up paying back the mortgage a little faster. Since there are more than four weeks in a month, you actually end up making the equivalent of thirteen monthly payments every year instead of twelve."

Pulling a computer printout from my pocket, I resumed. "If you had a typical twenty-five-year, $100,000 mortgage at ten percent interest, and **paid it weekly or bi-weekly instead of monthly, you would save over $50,000 in interest** and have the mortgage paid off in less than nineteen years! That's a lot of money — for one small change in your mortgage. But the beauty of it is, since you pay only a little more every cheque, you don't even notice the difference. **Paying weekly or bi-weekly is a simple, painless way to cut your mortgage interest cost by about a third!**

"Another way to achieve the same thing is to make normal monthly payments, but take a shorter amortization period. If you took a nineteen-year mortgage and made monthly payments, you would save the same $50,000 in interest. That's why if you don't want to pay weekly or bi-weekly because you are paid once a month, you should take a fifteen- or twenty-year amortization period — whatever you can afford."

"Saving a third on your mortgage interest is fantastic," Scott conceded, "especially when it saves you tens of thousands of dollars. But you said there was a way to cut your mortgage cost in half. How do you do that?"

"There is a better way to lower your mortgage costs, even better than paying weekly or reducing your amortization period. And it gives you the best of both worlds — the lowest possible payments at the start when every penny counts, and a way to save the most interest, *without* sacrificing your standard of living at all."

"Dreamer! We wish," Rob, the skeptic, muttered.

"I've figured it out!" Scott jumped in. "You get someone else to make your mortgage payments," he said sarcastically, frustrated with my delay in getting to the bottom line.

"It can be done, and without someone else making your payments," I promised. "It's very simple. To get the lowest possible payment at the start, you need the longest amortization period — twenty-five years. Then, to cut your interest costs without lowering your standard of living, you simply **increase your payments every year as your income rises** with inflation. The additional money coming in from a raise covers the slightly higher mortgage payment without you giving up a thing.

"Since practically all mortgages allow you to increase your payments by at least ten percent each year, this strategy is available to everyone. The only problem with this approach is that it's not automatic, like paying weekly, or shortening your amortization period. If you want to pay as little interest as possible, with the least impact on your standard of living, you have to implement this strategy yourself.

"People don't think of doing something like this because lenders don't offer an automatic accelerated payment plan. And those who want to do it on their own might not remember to increase their payments every year. Others might not have the discipline."

"Let me see if I've got this," Scott began. "All you do is start with a normal twenty-five-year mortgage, and increase your payments each year as your income goes up?"

"That's it."

"And that cuts your mortgage interest cost in half?" he asked, unconvinced.

"That depends on how much you increase your payments each year," I said, again referring to my printout. "If you take a twenty-five-year, $100,000, twelve percent mortgage and **increase your payments by five percent each year, you will cut your total interest cost in half and save over $105,000** — *and* you can burn the mortgage in a little over twelve years!"

"Didn't your lender explain this to you?" Scott asked Rob.

"I wish! He didn't even tell me I should be paying biweekly," Rob snapped back.

"But most people's wages don't go up five percent or more like they used to," Scott objected. "Inflation has really come down lately."

"That's true," I admitted. "Some people might not be able to increase their payments five percent every year. An even easier way to cut the total interest cost of a twenty-five-year mortgage in half is to simply **pay weekly** instead of monthly, and **increase your payments each year by only two percent**. Even if you think inflation will average less than that, do you think you'd notice a payment increase of just two percent?"

"You're really into this money stuff, aren't you, Talbot?" Rob commented.

"I don't know," I responded. "I've just been trying to understand the basics, and not blindly rely on others. The truth is, no one cares more about your money than you do — except maybe those you owe money to." The guys obviously *owed* money, as this last comment drew a few laughs.

"Some people spend more time planning a vacation than they do planning their financial future. Yet the vacation lasts a few weeks, and your future is the rest of your life," I reflected.

"But it's tough to think about planning for retirement when it's so far away," Scott noted.

"Especially for someone who can't plan past next Saturday!" Rob quipped.

"Listen, while I'm thinking about it," I carried on, "do any of you guys know how to earn over twenty-five percent interest guaranteed?"

"Are you kidding?" Pierre gasped. "You can't even get ten percent. How do you expect to earn over twenty-five percent?"

"I don't know. I was hoping you knew," I said. "I'm pretty sure it's possible though, because I met a retired financial planner who said it was. But she didn't tell me how, and I won't be able to find out until she gets back after Christmas. If anybody does find out, let me know. Not only do I want to take advantage of it, she kind of expected that I would figure it out.

"Well, that's it for me," I announced, noting the time. "I've got a busy day tomorrow. If things go well, we'll be making an offer on a house."

"Talbot, before you go, have you figured out whether it's better to take a five-year term or a shorter one-year term?" Rob asked. "Like I told you, our mortgage is up for renewal soon."

"No, I haven't thought about that," I admitted. "But I guess it applies to us as well. I'll see if I have time to look into it and we can talk about it next week."

★ ★ ★

"Congratulations! So you started a 'leveraged forced savings plan', eh?" Scott mimicked, as we met at the arena the next Saturday.

"Yeah, we did. We closed the deal on a house in the north end, minutes from the school. We move in at the end of October, a month before Theresa is due."

"That's good. That'll give you some time to get settled before the baby comes — and life as you know it changes forever." Rob's encouragement was sometimes too much.

The hour of hockey was much easier to take this week. The inner thighs and lungs were much more enthusiastic about participating.

Afterwards, we relived missed opportunities for glory, and enjoyed watching the new crop of faces. With September bringing the students back to town, the bar was packed with kids lusting for excitement.

"Hey, Talbot, did you figure out whether you're going to get a long- or short-term mortgage?" Rob asked.

"Yeah, I did."

"Well?"

"Well, I found out that most of the time, interest rates for five-year terms are higher than rates for one-year terms by about one to two percent. That means you generally pay extra to have the security of locking in a rate for the longer term."

"But it's a lot easier to sleep at night knowing that your biggest monthly expense — your mortgage payment — won't go up for five years," Rob countered.

"There's no doubt about it," I agreed. "By locking in your rate for five years, you don't have to worry about losing the house. If you can afford the payments at the start, it should only get easier for you as your income rises. If it's important for your peace of mind to know your payments are fixed for five years, then definitely take the longer term," I said, and hesitated for a second.

"But?" Scott prodded. He knew me well enough to know there was more.

"But, you have to realize how much of a premium you pay for that security. Paying a higher rate for a longer term is like buying insurance. If the rates go up, you're protected. But if rates go down, not only can't you get the lower rate, you've paid all that insurance premium — the higher interest rate — for nothing.

"As I noted, short-term rates are usually at least one percent lower than five-year rates. Right now, one-year rates are *two* percent lower. If half a percent lower can save you a couple thousand dollars, then getting a rate that is two percent less will save you that much more.

"Since we're going to be borrowing about $100,000, the two-percent-lower rate will save us more than $1,600 in payments each year," I added, while signalling Phil for another round of refreshments.

"But at the end of the year, the rates could be up," Rob again expressed his concern.

"True," I admitted. "I don't know which way rates will go. But I do know that they'll have to go up at least two percent in the next year before we *start* paying as much as someone who took the five-year term."

"And, since no one knows where rates are going," Pierre added, "you've got a fifty-fifty chance that rates will be down in a year. Then the person with the one-year term is even further ahead."

"That's true, too," I agreed. "But the reason we're comfortable taking the one-year term is because Theresa and I didn't go out and get the biggest house that the lenders would let us buy. Since we can comfortably make the payments even if rates do go up, we know we're not going to lose the house."

"I've always taken a one-year term," Pierre remarked, "and the years that one-year rates were high, the five-year rates were even higher."

"Well, I think I'm still going with the five-year term," Rob announced. "I know I could probably save some money doing what you guys are doing. But with money so tight and not knowing when I'll get back to work, I can't afford to take the chance."

"That's fine," I reassured. "As in any decision, you shouldn't do something that makes you uncomfortable. Scott, I found out something else that should interest you since you might be in the same boat I'm in. You know that if you don't have a twenty-five percent down payment, the lender will tell you that you have to pay up to two-and-a-half percent extra to insure the mortgage?"

"No, but I'll take your word for it."

"Well, first of all, the insurance is of no value to you at all. It's to protect the lender, so that if you default on your payments, they are guaranteed to be paid in full.

But the interesting thing is that that's not your only option. Let's say you needed another $15,000 to end up with a twenty-five percent down payment. The other option, which our banker never told us about, was that we could borrow the $15,000 as a second mortgage at a slightly higher rate. That way, we wouldn't have to pay this extra mortgage payment insurance.

"Our broker says that if we can pay off the small second mortgage in five or six years, then we would come out further ahead than paying extra to get an insured first mortgage."

"And an even better way to go," Pierre added, "is to borrow the $15,000 from a relative and pay them a lower rate. Since people often don't declare the interest for tax purposes, both the lender and the borrower come out ahead."

"But you're supposed to pay tax on the interest, aren't you?" Scott asked.

"Of course," he answered. "I didn't say it was right, just that some people do it."

"Do you have any relatives who can lend you $15,000?" Scott asked me.

"No."

"I told you you should have married rich!"

"Now you tell me!" I played along with him. "But if I did know someone with money, I would recommend that they declare the interest on the loan, just the same."

"You're too honest!" Pierre accused in a disappointed tone.

"Don't kid yourself, Pierre," Scott said with a smirk. "You obviously don't know him very well. Have you ever played cards with this guy?"

"No, wh—"

"Don't listen to these guys," I butted in quickly, trying not to let the opinion of a few guys that have been drinking cloud the truth. "I've never cheated at cards in my life. Why, I'm as honest as the day is long."

"Oh?" Rob joined the coalition. "Well, that explains it then, with winter coming and the days getting shorter. Did we mention that he lies too?"

Although the guys' laughter was definitely at my expense, I laughed along with them, before resuming. "That reminds me. You guys know that I recently bought a minivan and took out a loan for it."

"Yeah."

"Well, I just discovered **a way that a lot of people can lower their personal loan payments**, without —"

"Excuse me, Talbot," Phil, the bartender, interrupted. "You're wanted on the phone."

Who would call me at the bar, at this time of night? When I hung up the phone, I immediately put on my coat and headed for the door.

"Where are you going?"

"I've got a personal emergency at home. That was Theresa. She said if I didn't get home immediately, she was going to kill George."

After absorbing what I had said, Scott asked the obvious. "Who's George?" They were all probably thinking that Theresa's pregnancy had turned her homicidal.

"It's not what you think," I quickly dispelled their fears. "George is the name she gave my new computer. She has to get a report prepared for Monday and she doesn't get along with computers very well. She lost over three hour's work, and is threatening to teach George skydiving from our balcony — and we live on the ninth floor!

"We'll see you guys next week. See you at work on Monday, Pierre." And I was off to save my computer.

⊲ 8 ⊳
Good Consumers Get
More for Less

"So, did you save George?" Scott asked, as we settled down at our favourite watering hole in front of the Leafs game. The week had gone by so quickly that I barely remembered the emergency seven days earlier.

"Yeah," I recalled. "I got home in time to prevent Theresa from hurting the computer. I wasn't really worried about her throwing it out the window — it's too heavy for that. But she was pretty upset about losing her file. When I heard some of the words she was using, I had to compliment her on being such a quick study in the one language that all programmers know — profanity!

"I consoled her with the fact that everyone has frustrating days with computers, and that the machines instantly do what you tell them to do. All you have to do is tell them exactly what you want. She warned that that would be difficult to get used to since, as a married woman, she wasn't used to immediately getting exactly what she asked for!"

"So, are she and George speaking again?"

"Yeah. She was pretty relieved to find out that I could recover her lost file, and decided to forgive it."

"So, anyway," Rob started, "what were you saying last week about reducing personal loans?"

"Well, I was reading this newspaper article a few weeks ago," I replied, "that said when it comes to buying smart, we really fail. It talked about how North Americans not only know almost nothing about investing, but also fail miserably as consumers.

"The article claimed that even educated people knew very little about things like buying a house, insurance, a car, bank accounts, even everyday shopping. In the last few months, I've proven that I was ignorant about insurance, buying a car, and mortgages. Now that I understand a few basics, we've saved thousands of dollars and will continue to in the future."

"So, is that where you learned how to save money on personal loans?" Rob asked.

"Basically. The article didn't go into a lot of details and mostly talked about how much our lack of knowledge was costing us. But it did point out some other areas where we might be making costly mistakes."

"Such as?" Scott was prompting me now.

"It said that people don't realize they can refinance fixed-rate personal loans, that we unnecessarily spend money on low-value extended warranties, and often have the wrong type of bank services."

"So how does refinancing a fixed-rate loan save you money? There must be penalties to pay just like mortgages," Rob assumed.

"That's what I thought, too," I replied. "After I read the article, I talked to our loan manager. I found out that there are **generally no penalties to refinance fixed-rate personal loans**. He pointed out that not very many people are aware of that, and it obviously wasn't in his best interest to go around telling everyone.

"So when interest rates drop one or two percent, you should take ten minutes to get your banker or car dealership to refinance at the lower rate. If the lender doesn't want to, simply tell them you can get cheaper money from any of their competitors to pay off the loan — if they wish."

"And interest rates have dropped a lot in the last year or so," Pierre pointed out.

"I know. That means you'll save even more by refinancing. I figured out that if you borrowed $10,000 to buy a car a year ago when rates were three percent higher, refinancing at today's rates would save over $400 during the last three years of the four-year loan."

"That's it? All I have to do is tell the bank that I want today's lower interest rate? It almost sounds too easy." Rob was impressed by how simple it was to lower his debt costs.

"Knowing that you can refinance personal loans without penalty is pretty valuable when rates have dropped. The way fixed-rate loans are set up, the consumer wins no matter which way rates go. You get protection against rates going up, as well as the ability to refinance at lower rates without penalty if they go down," I summarized.

"But that doesn't help you much," Scott said. "You just got your loan for the van a month ago."

"That's true. Interest rates haven't dropped since we got the van. But they are lower than when we took out our student loans. And instead of lowering our payments, we're still paying the same amount so the loans will be paid off months earlier."

"That's a good idea," Pierre added, agreeing with the approach. "If you can afford the payments now, then why not use the opportunity to pay off your debts that much faster."

"That's what we thought, so we did it," I said. "But we benefited even more when I read the van's loan agreement and discovered I had made a mistake — and I should have known better. Rob, when we were talking about getting the van, didn't you say to stay away from the life and disability insurance the lenders try to sell?"

"Yeah, I think so. It's a really overpriced option that just adds to the lender's profit."

"That's what I thought, and if you're already properly insured, there's even less reason to get it. Well, I didn't listen very well. When I read the loan agreement, I discovered that in the excitement of getting our first 'new' car, somehow we had agreed to the loan insurance that cost $340."

"You should be able to cancel that," Pierre advised. "My brother made that mistake once and he was able to get his money back."

"I know. I explained the mistake to our banker, and that we didn't want the overpriced insurance. Then he did something that really surprised me."

"What's that?"

"He said that since the loan was only a month old and it was possible that he didn't take the time to explain it clearly, he was going to give us a full refund!"

"And you thought all bankers were bad," Scott remarked.

"I guess he knows how to keep a customer happy. I know it would have been better to apply the refund against the loan to save a payment or two, but with the extra bills setting up the house and Christmas coming, it was nice to have the extra cash. Theresa and I have been trying to get most of the shopping done before she has the baby."

"So how is your better half?" Rob asked.

"Don't you mean his *better three-quarters?*" Scott corrected.

"She's fine," I smiled and shook my head at Scott's remark. "Except for a little lower back discomfort, she's very healthy. Of course, if I had to carry around an extra twenty-five pounds all day, I'd probably have some back pain too. We almost have everything ready to move into the house on the 25th. Rob, you still able to help move?"

"Sure, what are friends for?"

"Do you need an extra hand?" Pierre volunteered.

"Thanks, Pierre. Beer and pizza's on the house — no pun intended."

"I'd help too, but I'm working that day," Scott claimed.

"I know," I sighed, exaggerating my disappointment. "Don't worry, we'll get you next time."

"Anyway, I was going to mention that when I was in the bank, I also looked into the types of accounts and services that were available." I paused a few seconds to watch a replay of Lemieux scoring his second goal against the Leafs.

"And?"

"And the first thing I learned was that we had the wrong type of bank accounts. Until a few weeks ago, we had a regular chequing account to write cheques, and an investment savings account for those few times that there was a little extra cash. But by switching to a single investment chequing account that pays interest, I figured out that we should gain about fifty dollars a year, whether our balance is six hundred or six thousand.

"Not only will one account save us money, it's also much easier to manage. All transactions — money in and out, cheques, and pre-authorized withdrawals — are all detailed on one monthly statement. And we don't have to make any more special trips to the bank to move money to the chequing account to make sure that cheques are covered."

"That really doesn't apply to me," Rob said. "We only have a chequing account and it rarely has any money in it."

"What's more important," I resumed, "was that I realized we were getting almost no value from the service plan that was costing us over a hundred dollars a year. When we first started the plan, it sounded good and only cost eight dollars a month."

"You know why businesses break the cost down into tiny pieces — only eight dollars a month, only pennies a day?" Rob asked, rhetorically. "So you don't think it costs that much. If they can make the cost *seem* small enough, people will buy. Consumers never bother to add up the total cost. In sales we use it all the time, and it works like a charm."

"Well, that's exactly what happened to us," I went on. "When I realized we were paying over a hundred dollars a year, I took a closer look at what we were getting for that money, and what services we really needed. The only service we were getting any benefit from was the so-called 'free' chequing. But how can anyone call something 'free' when you're paying a hundred bucks a year for it! And you know that saving a hundred dollars is the same as earning an extra two hundred."

"Why's that?" Rob asked, looking surprised.

"With taxes and all of the other deductions that come off your cheque, you need to make almost two dollars to end up with one. So saving one dollar is the same as earning two. That's why **shopping around is so important**. If you can get the same TV for a hundred less by making a few calls or shopping at a discount store, then that's the same as working an extra shift for two hundred dollars.

"Even when you save a dollar, you actually end up saving more than a dollar. In Ontario, because of the eight percent PST and seven percent GST, saving a dollar is really saving $1.15."

"I read that the nineties is the decade of the value-conscious consumer," Scott added.

"That's what I heard," Pierre agreed. "The eighties was the decade for spenders. The nineties is the decade for savers. Now that everyone realizes there might not be much of a Canada Pension Plan left for our retirement, people are saving more to take care of their own futures."

"And there's a —"

"Talking about retirement, what about RRSPs?" Scott interrupted. "People who have RRSPs say they're the best thing since sliced bread, but I really don't know that much about them."

"I don't have any, or know much about them either — yet," I admitted. "But I'm going to find out why they're so popular after Christmas, before the RRSP deadline at the end of February.

"Before I was so rudely interrupted," I jokingly teased Scott, "I was going to say that there's a difference between being cheap and being thrifty. Thrifty people buy exactly what they want — but get it for less. The cheap person doesn't want to buy anything because it costs money. These days, being thrifty is a compliment. It means you know how to manage your money efficiently."

"Don't worry, Talbot. We know you're not cheap," Rob consoled. "You're always buying us something for one bet or another!"

"There are other ways to get the same thing for less," Pierre announced.

"How?" I asked, always willing to learn new ways to cut costs.

"By buying used instead of new. A lot of times you can find cars, appliances, and furniture practically new — for a fraction of the price."

"I know that now. Thanks to Rob we bought a one-year-old minivan instead of a new one and saved $6,000 — which, of course, is the same as a $12,000 raise."

"Another way to get things at **big discounts is at auctions**," Pierre noted. "Fortunately for me, most people don't know you can get new and used products at auctions and save as much as eighty percent. And I figure the fewer people that know about auctions, the better. That way there are fewer people bidding up the prices."

"I guess there are always companies going out of business," Rob reasoned, "and when they do, they're forced to liquidate to get what they can."

"It happens all the time," Pierre acknowledged, "and naturally there are even more auctions during recessions. When I wanted a bedroom suite, I watched the Saturday newspapers for auctions selling furniture, and picked up a brand-new oak bedroom suite for about a thousand less than the same one in a retail store. I did the same thing to get a dining room set to save another five hundred. Of course," he hung his head, "the ex has them now."

"Talking about furniture reminds me of something else mentioned in that article," I remembered. "It claimed that most of the time, extended warranties are a waste of money. Again, thanks to Rob, I know that's true for extended warranties on cars, but it's probably true for a lot of other products as well."

"I remember when we bought our living room set right after getting married, the salesman couldn't understand why we didn't want to spend an extra $150 for the extended warranty and fabric protection. He tried so hard to sell it to us, I knew it had to be a bad deal. We ended up spending fifteen dollars for a couple of cans of fabric protectant and did it ourselves. What's the story, Rob? You sold appliances. Do extended warranties make sense?"

"Yeah, they make sense — but for the company, not the consumer," Rob admitted. "Like overpriced options on a car, extended warranties are an easy way for the seller to make extra profit. Most people don't think about the extra cost, only the security of having the longer warranty. But if there is a problem, it usually happens within the first year and is covered by the manufacturer's warranty. And most of the things that go wrong after the manufacturer's warranty expires are due to normal wear and tear — which isn't covered. Of course, you didn't hear any of this from me. I don't want to ruin any chance on being called back to my old job."

"We understand," Scott smiled. "But why didn't you tell us this before? A couple of years ago, I learned about extended warranties the hard way. When some stitching started coming apart on my couch, the company claimed that it was from normal use and they couldn't do anything about it."

"If you want to cancel, you might be able to get a refund on the unused portion of the warranty," Rob suggested. "Give the company a call and find out."

"I'll do that," Scott agreed. "I guess it never hurts to try."

★ ★ ★

"Talbot, where's your Christmas list?" Theresa asked. "Your mom's been asking for it." Kim and her daughter Rachel were over and the three of them were going shopping.

I had to admit that I *was* guilty of still making Christmas lists, but not to send off to Santa Claus like you did when you were a kid. I gave out Christmas lists to family — the real Santa Claus — who had the difficult task of buying a gift for a man. By giving them a list of inexpensive items that I *wanted*, and maybe even needed, I saved them hours of wandering through malls trying to think of something that might actually get used.

This also saved me from having to buy things I was going to get anyway, and more importantly, prevented the dreaded annual event where I hold up yet another yellow and purple sweater three sizes too big, paste a fake smile on my face and lie, "Thanks a lot. It's just what I needed!"

Seeing Kim finish a cigarette, I asked, "Kim, have you seen my new computer yet?"

"No, why?"

"Well, come and take a look. I want to show you something you should find interesting. I know you've tried to quit smoking before and that you want to quit. But, for whatever reason, you haven't found a way to do it yet. I'm sure you're well aware of what smoking does to your physical health, but you might not be aware of how smoking affects your financial health.

"I was using this new financial program the other day and I started playing with some numbers. Do you still smoke about a pack a day?" I asked.

"Yeah, about that."

"And a pack of cigarettes cost about ...?"

"About three dollars a pack," she replied. "More in some provinces."

"Call it three dollars. I also read an article that said the price of cigarettes went up almost fifteen percent per year through the eighties," I went on. "But for simplicity, let's assume that the cost of cigarettes goes up only ten percent a year."

"Alright."

"How much do you think it will cost you to continue smoking only one pack of cigarettes a day, say to age sixty-five?" I punched in the numbers and paused before showing the results on the screen.

"I don't know. You know I don't like math. Probably a couple hundred thousand," she guessed.

"What if I proved to you that you could be worth $500,000 by age sixty-five, just by quitting smoking — by not doing something you don't want to do anyway? Would that help you decide to quit?"

"Of course, I wouldn't have to worry about retirement then. But it can't cost that much to smoke," she stated confidently.

I pressed a key to display the results and explained. "**If you invested the cost of one pack of cigarettes a day at ten percent interest, forty years from now you would have $1,800,000!**"

Kim's disbelief silenced her for a few seconds. "That can't be right!"

"Fortunately, it is. I didn't believe it at first either. But I checked it three times."

"That's amazing! Almost two million dollars!" she gasped. Saying the amount out loud made it seem a little more real for her. "That's a lot of money."

"Would you be excited if you won a million dollars in a lottery the day you retired?" I asked rhetorically. "Now you know of a million dollar payoff you are guaranteed to win — just by giving up something that you want to stop anyway. Not only that, but by giving up smoking, you'll probably live long enough to enjoy spending it!"

She stared, glassy-eyed, at the screen. Knowing Kim, she was probably dreaming about the wonderful trips she could afford with that much money at retirement. "I know that you and Theresa have tried to help me stop smoking in the past, but this is a BIG reason to quit. I'm going to seriously think about it."

"Rachel would like it if you did," I said, reminding her that there were more important reasons to quit than money.

"I know."

★ ★ ★

The next few weeks were the most exciting of my life and passed quickly. Not long after we settled into our new home, Theresa gave birth to a healthy, bouncing, baby boy. One of Theresa's friends from work, a die-hard feminist, immediately consoled her by saying, "That's okay. Maybe you'll get it right next time!"

With the delivery late Tuesday night, the guys were surprised to see me show up at Kool's after hockey on Saturday.

"Congratulations!" everyone shouted.

"What are you doing here? When you missed hockey, we were sure you were at home up to your elbows in dirty diapers," Scott confessed.

"Theresa is recovering well and seems to have every-thing under control. I didn't want you guys to think that having a baby was going to totally change my life."

"Don't worry, I promise you — it will!" Rob warned, speaking from experience.

"Let me buy you a beer," Scott offered, "to celebrate the arrival of another Stevens boy."

"Thanks, Scott. Now I know how to get you to buy *me* a beer — all I have to do is have a baby!" I kidded.

"So you named him Derek," said Pierre. "Did you think about naming him Talbot Jr.?"

"No. I've never met another Talbot in my life and I wanted to keep it that way."

"Good thinking. One of you is more than enough!" Rob joked.

"So how was the delivery? Was it fun?" asked Pierre.

"Everything went fine. Theresa did really well and didn't swear or try to hit me or anything. But I was a little curious why there were so many people in the delivery room to catch one baby. Aside from Theresa and I, there were three doctors and a nurse.

The way I saw it from the head of the bed, the intern was the catcher, the senior resident was the umpire, and the consulting doctor was the backup umpire — just in case there were any close calls — with the nurse batting cleanup. When I asked the nurse why so many people were needed, she said the theory is that if there are enough people at the end of the bed, the baby won't hit the floor!

"Anyway, enough about me. What's new with you guys?"

"Well, you're not going to believe this," Rob hesitated, "but you know how you hear about these vacuum salesmen that come to your door . . ."

"I don't like the sound of this," Scott whispered.

"Yesterday, because we've been needing a new machine and they promised to clean a room for free, we let one in."

"You didn't buy one?" I hoped.

"We didn't plan on it. But after the salesman showed how it could do almost everything but wash the dishes . . . and that he was able to give us financing with easy, low payments that didn't start for nine months, we decided to make it our Christmas gift to each other." Rob paused, almost embarrassed by what had happened. "But today, after thinking about it, I don't know if it was such a great idea."

"How much did you pay for it?" I was almost afraid to ask.

"Twelve hundred dollars," Rob admitted reluctantly.

"Twelve hundred!" I echoed in disbelief. "You can buy a car for that!"

"I know it's too much to pay . . . now. But after all the trouble we had with the last machine, we didn't think about the twelve hundred — only the forty dollars a month. And when he said there were no payments for almost a year, I was certain I would have a job again before the payments started. But now I'm not so sure. As I said, I realize it was a mistake, but there's nothing I can do about it now."

"Yes there is," Pierre leapt in.

"What? We already signed a contract."

"The salesman came to your door yesterday, right?"

"Yeah."

"Well, if I remember my high school law class correctly," Pierre reflected, "there is a forty-eight hour 'cooling off' period for any contract that results from an unsolicited salesperson coming to your door. It's designed to protect people from being pressured into buying something they normally wouldn't."

"So, I can get out of the contract?" Rob hoped.

"You should be able to," replied Pierre. "I would call the company's sales manager first thing Monday morning, explain the situation, and tell him that you want out of the contract. I'd also send the company a letter by registered mail so there's a record of when it was sent, just in case. It's easy to dispute when a phone call took place, but no one can argue with physical proof, like a registered letter."

"If you really did want to buy the vacuum, however," Pierre added, "you probably **could have knocked a couple of hundred off the price just by negotiating**. I don't know why, but in Canada, everyone seems to automatically pay whatever is printed on a price tag. In many parts of the world, a price tag is just the starting point for negotiations."

"Yeah, I noticed that," Scott, the traveller, added. "And in some countries, they don't even put a price on things."

"You have to remember the golden rule," Pierre continued. "The one with the gold makes the rules. As long as your money is in your pocket, you are in control. And negotiating doesn't just apply to big purchases or where there's a large commission that the salesperson can take a cut on. It applies to most things.

"When I buy clothes, I ask the manager if I can get ten dollars off if I buy the third pair of pants. I let them know I can get the same thing at a competitor's store, but I'd just as soon get it here, now — *if* I can get a good deal. Sometimes they give me the discount and sometimes they don't. But there isn't an easier way to make ten dollars in thirty seconds, and it's fun! If they can't give you a discount, maybe they can throw in something small for free. It doesn't cost anything to try."

"I'll have to try that." I nodded. "It helps to know little ways to stretch your dollar. With the cost of living going up every year, money doesn't go as far as it used to — but it sure goes faster! I've learned a few more things in the last few weeks that should save you guys some money in the future, especially you, Scott."

"What?"

"I read in a magazine the other day that you can save hundreds of dollars on real estate transactions, simply by calling a toll-free number. Scott, have you contacted an agent to look for a house yet?"

"No, why?"

"Good. There's this organization called the **Canadian Transfer Association** that, among other things, can get you a guaranteed rebate when you buy or sell a house. All you have to do is call them before you contact your real estate agent. Let them know what agent you would like — or they can recommend one if you want — and everything else works as normal. To locate a guaranteed client, the agent gladly pays CTA's referring realtor a part of the commission, some of which is returned to you. That's how you get the rebate."

"So how much is the rebate?"

"A few weeks after closing, they'll send you a cheque for 0.3 percent of the total transaction, or three dollars for every thousand."

"So if I buy a $100,000 house, I'll get a cheque for $300 — just for making a phone call?" Scott asked for clarification.

"It's almost too easy, isn't it. And if you sold a $100,000 house to upgrade to a $200,000 house, you would get $900 back."

"You got their phone number?" Scott demanded.

"I thought you'd want to know, so I wrote it down. The number is **1-800-465-1198**. But don't you want to know the bad thing about the Canadian Transfer Association?" I asked.

"What's that?"

"The bad thing is that I didn't learn about it six months ago — before we bought our house!"

"But now you'll know for the next time," Scott consoled, grinning because for once his procrastination had paid off.

"There's something else you guys might want to try when you sell your house," Pierre added. "You know when someone uses a real estate agent, the seller pays a six percent commission to the agent?"

"No kidding!" Rob shouted. "The seller loses six percent right off the top. And on a house like ours, that can add up to almost ten thousand dollars."

"Yeah, it's a lot of money to sell something," Pierre conceded. "But it doesn't have to cost you that kind of money to sell a house. Most of the time, it does make sense to hire an agent's expertise to sell a house at the right price, but I know two friends who sold their homes themselves and saved eight or nine thousand dollars in commissions."

"They must have had buyers already lined up or something," Rob argued.

"No. They figured that since they weren't in a hurry, they would try to sell it themselves. It really doesn't take that much money to put up a sign, place a few ads in the paper and get the word out. Bigger newspapers have special home seller's editions where you can take out an advertisement with a picture of the house. There are even books on how to sell a house yourself."

"That's certainly something to consider," I agreed, "especially if the market is strong and you're not in a hurry to sell. Anyway, I should get back and see how Theresa is making out. I just wanted to stop by and let you guys know I'll be out for hockey next week for sure. Scott, are you and Kim still coming over for dinner next Friday night?"

"Yep."

"Good, because I'm cooking."

"You're kidding. . . . on second thought," Scott reflected, "I think Kim and I are busy that night. The last time you cooked, we sat down to lasagna and found out the hard way that you didn't know the difference between a *clove* of garlic and the entire bulb!"

"Hey, Scott, what's going on here? You're not still seeing Kim, are you?" Rob inquired. "This is a couple of months now. You'd better be careful or you might end up like one of us!"

The bachelor offered no reply to Rob's teasing.

"Talbot, did you ever find out how to earn that twenty-five percent interest guaranteed?" Pierre wondered.

"No, I didn't," I admitted. "But I'll find out soon. Sue, the retired financial planner, is returning from her trip after Christmas and she promised to tell me how, if I didn't already know."

⊲ 9 ⊳

Earn Over 25 Percent
Interest Guaranteed

Early in January, only a week after she was supposed
to be back from her six-month trip, I contacted Sue
Mitchell to find out her long-kept secret of how to earn
twenty-five percent interest guaranteed. In her friendly,
ever-helpful manner, she said she was willing to talk
about whatever I wanted — as long as I was buying. We
met the next night at a small family restaurant near her
house.

"So how have you been?" she asked.

"Great, yourself?"

"Good, I thought . . . until I went to the doctor for a
checkup. He thought I enjoyed myself too much while I
was away and suggested I go on a diet. He gave me a list
of everything I was supposed to eat for two weeks . . . .
But I think the doctor underestimated me," Sue said
frankly.

"Why, what do you mean?"

"Well, I was so efficient that I had eaten everything on
the list in the first three days!" Sue's carefree laughter
indicated that she wasn't worried about the few extra
pounds she had gained while away.

"So, how was Christmas here? I was in Australia at the
time. It sure is different celebrating Christmas with
koala bears in the eighty-degree heat."

"It was wonderful. My wife and I had our first baby, in
November. Having Derek around made Christmas a lot
more fun."

"Congratulations! Christmas is a lot more exciting with
kids around," Sue agreed.

"Yeah, all the relatives go crazy with gifts when you
have a baby. Derek's barely a month old and he already

owns more than his parents. We're even thinking about putting the mortgage in his name to get a better rate!" I joked. "So how was your trip?"

"It was my best ever," she declared with enthusiasm. "I spent most of my time in southern Europe, sunning on the beaches in Greece, snorkeling in the Mediterranean. Then, for a change in pace, I went skiing in the Swiss Alps. My last stop was a month in Australia. But it's summer there now and hot — too hot sometimes."

"I just got back from skiing with some buddies up in Collingwood, although I doubt that compares with the Swiss Alps." The adventures of my life seemed to pale against Sue's.

"I've been there," she remarked. "It's not bad, but if you get a chance, you should take your wife to France for some real skiing."

"Sue, you seem to forget that we're not made of money like you," I said enviously. "But we'd like to be. That's why I wanted to see you, to find out how to earn twenty-five percent interest guaranteed."

"You *will* have more money than you need," she stated, in a matter-of-fact manner that surprised me.

"Why do you say that?"

"Because you're learning how to manage your money, and you're doing it when you're young. Most people never learn the first thing about money until retirement, when it's too late. Then they discover they should have learned more decades earlier.

"I'll bet you've already learned a lot more than getting the right life insurance since we talked six months ago."

Sue was obviously a quick judge of character. "You're right," I replied. "After correcting my life insurance to save $900 a year, I found ways to lower our car and home insurance premiums as well. Then, when we went to buy a minivan, a friend showed us how to save $6,000 and get practically the same vehicle. But those savings are nothing compared to what I learned about mortgages. We should save at least a hundred thousand dollars in interest by paying bi-weekly and increasing our payments each year as our incomes go up.

"And you know the best thing about everything we've done to save money?" I asked.

"What?"

"It's all been done without any risk or sacrifice. We haven't had to give up a thing. Actually, with the savings from buying a one-year-old minivan instead of a new one, I was able to buy the brand-new computer I've been wanting for a long time!"

"You learned all that and didn't figure out how to earn a guaranteed twenty-five percent interest — even after the hint I gave you?" Sue seemed disappointed.

"What hint?"

"You remember how I said saving one dollar is the same as earning two . . ."

"Yeah."

". . . and that most people aren't aware of how taxes affect them, both as consumers *and* investors?"

"Not really."

"That was the clue that should have given it away," she said. I wasn't following, and it must have shown on my face. "Don't feel bad. I've met investors with hundreds of thousands of dollars who don't really understand how taxes affect their investments."

"I don't understand. The best guaranteed investments are paying less than ten percent interest. How can taxes give you a higher return? Paying taxes only lowers your —"

"Of course taxes don't increase your returns," Sue confirmed the obvious. "But *understanding* how taxes affect you can help you identify investments that do result in returns of twenty percent, thirty percent or even higher — *guaranteed*.

"Suppose you're in the middle tax bracket and buy a Guaranteed Investment Certificate that pays ten percent interest. Let's look at what really happens. At the end of the year, how much interest do you get?" she tested.

"Ten percent of the amount invested, of course." The answer seemed trivial.

"I wish it were true." Sue shook her head slowly. "In this country, when you buy a GIC that pays ten percent interest, you haven't made an investment that makes you ten percent. You've made an investment that makes six percent interest for you, and four percent for the government as income tax. You see, interest income, just like regular income, is taxed at your marginal tax rate."

"What's a *marginal tax rate?*"

"That's the percentage of income tax you would pay on your last dollar of income. Being in the middle income bracket, if you earned one extra dollar, you would pay more than forty percent of it to the government as federal and provincial income tax. But you already knew that. That's why a dollar saved is almost two dollars earned."

"It still hurts to think that when I earn a hundred dollars of interest, over forty percent of it goes to the government."

"Consider yourself fortunate," Sue said. "Those in the highest tax bracket pay over fifty percent tax on the last dollars they make."

"But how does knowing that get me an investment that pays over twenty-five percent interest?"

"I'm getting to that," she assured. "I'm trying to make sure that you fully understand the difference between *before-tax* returns and *after-tax* returns. As I said before, it's one of the most important concepts, yet most people aren't aware of it. So," she repeated, "what is your after-tax return from the ten percent GIC?"

"After paying taxes, I end up with only six percent, like you said."

"Right. So your ten percent before-tax return is really a six percent after-tax return. Remember, you're only interested in how much interest *you* earn, not how much you split with the government."

"You've got that right!" I agreed.

"Now let's turn it around for a second," Sue continued. "If you can find an investment that gives you an after-tax return of six percent, that's the same as getting a ten percent GIC, right?"

"Yeah."

"Let's double it now. If you could find an after-tax return of twelve percent, wouldn't that be the same as getting a before-tax return of twenty percent — in other words a twenty percent GIC?"

"Yeah," I said, starting to see where she was going. "But where can you get an after-tax return of twelve percent when you can't even find an investment that pays that much before tax?"

"You're only thinking of conventional investments that you buy from a bank or an investment broker," Sue sighed. "But there are many other ways to 'invest' your money. What interest rate are you paying on your mortgage?"

"Ten percent, why?"

"If you 'invested' a hundred dollars by paying down your mortgage balance, what kind of return on investment would you get?"

"Ten percent, I guess. I wouldn't have to pay ten percent interest on that hundred dollars any more, so I would get a ten percent return."

"That's partially right, but here's the clincher. Is that a ten percent *before-tax* return, or a ten percent *after-tax* return?"

"What do you mean? You don't have to pay any extra taxes to repay your debts," I replied, realizing I had answered my own question.

"Of course not," Sue confirmed. "Paying down debts results in an *after-tax* return. So paying down your ten percent mortgage is the same as earning a before-tax return of closer to seventeen percent."

"Let me make sure I understand. You're saying that if I could get a seventeen percent GIC, I'd be no further ahead than paying off my ten percent mortgage?"

"You got it," she affirmed. A smile swept my face as I finally understood. But there had to be more.

"Sue, seventeen percent is an excellent return, but you said that there was an investment that paid over twenty-five percent interest guaranteed."

"That's easy," she retorted. "Once you realize that paying off your mortgage debt is a great return, think about other debts that charge much more than mortgages. What about personal loans, car loans, and the most expensive of them all — credit cards. For someone in the middle tax bracket, **paying down a fifteen percent**

credit card is the same as getting a twenty-five percent GIC!"

"You're kidding!" It was still difficult to believe and took a few seconds to sink in.

"There's more," Sue resumed. "Not only does paying down your debts reduce stress and equate to getting a very high interest rate, the investment is guaranteed — and easy. Repaying part or all of a debt is guaranteed to save you the high after-tax interest charge. And in the case of credit cards, taking advantage of this 'investment' couldn't be easier since they send the application right to your door."

"What do you mean?"

"They mail you the credit card bill. All you have to do is fill in a payment amount higher than the minimum and you've guaranteed that some of your money will earn at least twenty-five percent interest. What could be easier than that?"

"Not much. I'm impressed! I have to admit that after not having any luck figuring it out, I was skeptical about your claim to be able to earn over twenty-five percent interest guaranteed," I confessed. "I was sure you were going to talk about an investment that *could* gain twenty-five percent or that had done well in the past, but wasn't a guaranteed twenty-five percent. That one word 'guaranteed' makes all the difference in the world."

"That's true," Sue agreed, "especially here in Canada where many people are either unaware or afraid of non-guaranteed investments and their potential for higher returns. But the fact is, I could have told you there was a way to earn over fifty percent interest guaranteed, at least for some people."

"But I never would have believed you," I told her frankly.

"I know. That's why I said 'over *twenty-five* percent interest guaranteed', and not a higher figure. If I told you that you could earn fifty percent interest guaranteed and left for six months without telling you how, you probably would have concluded I was just a senile old woman and never called me again.

"But some charge cards, such as those from department stores, charge as much as twenty-nine percent interest *after-tax!* And you probably didn't realize it, but these cards generally compound interest monthly instead of yearly. This means the effective annual interest rate is closer to thirty-three percent. By adding the two words 'compounded monthly' in fine print, the lender gets to charge you almost four percent more without you even knowing it!"

As I shook my head slowly, Sue continued. "That's why it's so important when you are comparing rates to find out what the compounding frequency is, and the real effective annual interest rate."

"So if department store cards charge a thirty-three percent after-tax interest rate, what is the equivalent before-tax rate?" my curiosity needed to know.

"It's the same as getting a GIC that pays fifty-five percent interest! Let me ask you something. How many fifty-five percent GICs have you seen lately? If banks offered a fifty-five percent GIC today, people would be lined up around the block to buy them. Ironically, many people could get that kind of return easily — if they only knew what you now know. Think about how many people have Canada Savings Bonds or GICs that pay single-digit rates while they pass up the opportunity to earn twenty-five, thirty-five, or even fifty-five percent interest guaranteed by paying down their credit cards."

I thought about our own situation a moment and admitted, "Guilty." When saving the down payment for our house, we had some Canada Savings Bonds and term deposits, but we left a balance on our credit cards.

"But it's so easy *not* to pay off your credit cards every month," I rationalized.

"Yes, I know," Sue agreed. "That's what makes them so dangerous. Because using plastic is so painless, many people can't resist purchasing things they wouldn't otherwise buy. It's too easy, especially for your generation, to think you can use credit to buy everything you want today and then worry about paying for it later. Some people seem to automatically expect to have their parents' standard of living the minute they leave home. They don't realize that their parents took twenty or thirty years to get to that point. . . . Sorry for the preaching. I'm not your mother."

"That's all right," I said. Although she was starting to sound like my parents, I had to admit that it was unreasonable to expect to have *everything* today. "At least now I know what it costs to use credit cards without paying them off. I guess we felt we were further ahead if we had some money in the bank. But thanks to you, now I know we were just fooling ourselves. So, should we cut up our credit cards?"

"No, not if you can control yourselves," she said. "They *are* convenient, and also a good deal if used properly. If you pay your card balance off in full every month, you get to use the bank's money for several weeks interest free. Actually, about half the people do exactly that, so they can't take advantage of this great investment."

"But that means that half the people *can* earn a high guaranteed return by paying down their credit cards," I noted, seeing the glass as half full instead of half empty. "More correctly, those that pay their cards off every month already are earning over twenty-five percent interest, and those that don't can start to."

"You're right," Sue concurred, "and most people have some kind of debt, at least a mortgage. Remember, for someone in the forty percent marginal tax bracket, paying down a ten percent mortgage is the same as getting a GIC that pays seventeen percent. That's a tough investment to beat.

"I should tell you though, that there is one other investment that is almost as good as paying down your expensive debts, and is available to practically everyone."

"What's that?"

"I'm not going to tell you what it is tonight," she teased, exposing her empty glass of wine.

"Why not? Why can't you tell me now?" I asked, wondering if this was the price to pay for letting her glass run dry.

She leaned back and smiled. "Did you ever notice that when you had to work really hard to achieve something, or when you made a really big mistake, you remember it for the rest of your life?"

I said nothing and listened.

"Many times, if something is just given to you, you not only don't appreciate it, you also don't realize its full value. Tell me, will you ever forget how to earn over twenty-five percent interest guaranteed? Not likely. Will you take advantage of it? Most definitely."

She paused, giving me time to absorb her wisdom.

"This also gives you another chance to figure it out on your own to redeem yourself. And besides, if you don't figure it out, it'll only cost you another dinner to find out!"

⊰ 10 ⊱
Ten Percent Magic

"Phil, let's have a beer here for the scoring machine, The Great One's twin brother, Rob Gretzky," Scott shouted as we entered Kool's to celebrate Rob's surprising hat trick. "For weeks the guy barely has a shot on net and all of a sudden he has three goals out of nowhere. Pierre, what do you have to say for yourself and tonight's sieve-like performance?" Scott teased.

"What's the big deal? It was just a practice. Besides, someone told me it was his birthday!" Pierre joked, hoping someone would believe him.

"Come on, you can do better than that!" Rob roared, disappointed with Pierre's feeble effort to vindicate himself. "I've seen you shut out everybody before, but tonight I had your number. I was hot."

"You did play well, and I didn't," Pierre admitted, turning to me. "So, Talbot, how is fatherhood treating you so far?" It was an obvious attempt to move to a different subject.

"Ah . . .," I hesitated. "I love it — most of the time. I'm still trying to get used to not getting a full night's sleep. And for Scott's sake, I won't mention what it's like to change a dozen dirty diapers everyday. But even though the most exciting thing Derek does is lift his head, it's worth it. Theresa's already forgotten about the delivery and says we can have another one . . . later."

"Hey, are you guys hungry?" Scott asked, as we jockeyed for a seat with a good view of a TV. "Why don't we split a Kitchen Sink Pizza?"

"A what?" a puzzled Pierre demanded. "Never mind. I'm not even going to ask what's in it. I'll just trust you guys — the first time."

"Don't worry," Scott assured him with a wink. "You'll love it."

"Did Talbot tell you guys about the seminar we went to last week?" asked Pierre.

"No, what was it about?"

"It was a financial seminar, about managing your money, investing, RRSPs, that sort of thing. I learned a lot and the speaker wasn't some boring finance type like I expected. The guy was actually pretty entertaining. I'm glad Talbot invited me along."

"How much did it cost?" Rob wondered.

"It was free."

"So, why didn't you tell us about it?" Scott grumbled.

"I didn't know you wanted to go," I apologized.

"So what was it about? Was it one of these 'get-rich-quick-in-real-estate-with-no-money-down' deals that you see on late-night TV?" Rob snickered.

"No," Pierre shook his head. "It was about a lot of simple, common-sense ways that average people like you and me can take control of our financial future.

"That's what the seminar made us realize. Do you know that half of retirees are dependent on the government? We need to take responsibility for our own future. And the speaker pointed out a couple of other reasons we might need more money than we think to retire comfortably.

"These days, a lot of people in their peak earning years are being forced to retire early because they are permanently laid off. Unless you are continually retraining to upgrade your skills, you could be one of them. Obviously, if you stop working ten years earlier than you had planned, you'll need a lot more money to live on."

"And some people might *want* to retire early," Scott was quick to add. "Like me."

"And as medical advances continue and people take better care of themselves, we're all living longer," Pierre noted. "Today, men can expect to live into their late seventies, and women even longer. The way our life expectancy has been increasing lately, who knows how long *we* will live? If technology adds another five years to your life, you're going to need even more money to maintain a comfortable lifestyle in retirement.

"Plus there's inflation. Although there's nothing you can do about it, inflation gives you all the more reason to save. If your retirement income stays the same while the cost of living goes up every year, you'd better either get used to the idea of trying to live on less or have a larger retirement fund."

"But how much money do *we* need to save for our retirement?" Scott asked. "Isn't that why we contribute to our company's pension plan?"

"That's what I thought, too," I answered. "But, do you know something? Most people don't have a pension. And those who do might be surprised at how little they'll get. Unfortunately, many people don't look at their pension plan until it's almost time to retire. But it's a little late to change much then. You should **take a look at your pension plan now** to find out what options you have. Until I talked to our personnel director, I wasn't aware that I could choose what type of investments my pension funds were in.

"And as for the Canada Pension Plan, most people know they can't count on it. By the time we retire, there'll be a zillion retirees, and fewer workers. So, CPP benefits are either going to be cut back, or the amount that workers will have to contribute will continue to increase every year. Either way, we lose. Besides, the way the government handles our money now, does it make sense to rely on them for our future finances?"

"Good point," Scott agreed. "The way the government debt keeps growing, they make *me* look like a good money manager! But how are we supposed to save for retirement when it's tough enough just trying to keep up with the bills? I know we need to save, but —"

"Using some of the things we learned at the workshop," Pierre interjected, "it's easy to take care of your retirement needs."

"How?" asked Rob. "We've tried budgeting to save before and it didn't last two months. There was never any money left over at the end of the month because we couldn't stand thinking about every purchase and wondering if the budget could afford it."

"I've never tried budgeting and I'm not going to," I declared. "Who wants to live in a financial straitjacket, especially when there is an easy, painless way to save?"

"What do you mean 'painless'?"

"I mean an automatic way to save that takes no effort, so you don't even notice you're doing it."

"Go away!" Rob protested in disbelief.

"It's true," Pierre assured. "You remember how you can save thousands on mortgage interest simply by paying weekly or reducing your amortization period? Those plans work well because they automatically commit you to pay your mortgage back a little bit faster than you normally would. Because it's such a small difference, you don't even notice. Two months after you start, you don't even remember you're doing it."

"So what does that have to do with saving money for retirement?"

"So," I took over, "if you could set up a similar system where a small amount of your paycheque is automatically invested *before* you get it, you get the same benefits. And again, because it's only a small amount, you don't even miss the money. But over time, those small regular investments grow to unbelievable sums. There's no need for a budget to save because, by paying yourself first instead of last, your long-term needs are automatically taken care of."

"That's nothing new," Scott scoffed. "Everyone's heard of 'pay yourself first'."

"Sure," I agreed. "Many people have heard: 'Pay yourself first. Invest ten percent of your income'. But how many have actually done it? Being aware of something and benefiting from it are often two different things. Many people receive advice, but only the wise profit from it. Last summer, several financial planners offered me the advice to pay myself first, but I didn't listen. I guess I felt that we couldn't afford it, or that our small ten percent wouldn't amount to much.

"But that was before the seminar the other night. After reading most of the book that I picked up, I have to agree

with the speaker that '**paying yourself first ten percent of your income**' is the most valuable financial
advice you could ever act on.

"The plan's strength lies in the fact that it's easy. Ten
minutes is all it takes to set it up. Either get your employer to take ten percent off the top of your cheque, or go
to any financial institution and get them to set up a Pre-
Authorized Chequing or PAC plan. Either way, the
money is automatically moved to a separate account
before you see it. And it's tough to spend what you don't
see."

"Not for *my* wife!" Rob protested.

"And the best part is that paying yourself first involves
no noticeable sacrifice," Pierre added, ignoring Rob. "A
few months after you set it up, you will have forgotten
you've done it. A guy at work told me he started paying
himself first a little more than ten percent of his net
income five years ago. To see if putting aside ten percent
had any noticeable impact on their lifestyle, he set up a
PAC plan — but didn't tell his wife who paid most of the
household bills.

"A year after starting, his wife still hadn't noticed the
difference — until he took *some* of the money and surprised her with a two-week vacation in the Bahamas!
Since she never missed the money, she felt it was a free
vacation. She was so elated with the pay-yourself-first
approach, she started her own ten percent fund. Now,
every other year, they reward themselves with a nice
vacation while the rest of their funds keep growing for
retirement."

"But I'd never survive on ten percent less," Scott, who
once defined expenses as 110 percent of his income, con-
tended.

"You wouldn't?" Rob huffed, not very sympathetic to
Scott's financial hardships. "You've got a job!"

"You two might find this hard to believe at first,"
Pierre declared, "but it really doesn't matter what your
income level is to benefit from paying yourself ten percent. Think about what happens when your employer
starts making deductions from your paycheque for things
like union dues, pension contributions, or charitable

donations. Sure, you notice initially, mostly because they told you about it. But soon after they start, you completely forget about it."

"Oh, yeah?" Rob challenged. "You might not notice ten percent off *your* paycheque. But if I deposited ten percent of my UIC cheque, I'd notice all right — when my mortgage cheque bounced, or when we didn't have enough money left to buy food."

"That may be so, now," Pierre said, "when your income is lower than it normally is. "But if you think that ten percent is too much, you might start by putting aside only five percent. The **important thing** isn't so much to invest ten percent as getting started — **setting aside some amount on a regular basis and not touching it.**"

"The thing that I like the most," I helped out, "is that it's automatic, and doesn't take any effort. Once you set up a pay-yourself-first plan and forget about it, you can be the worst money manager in the world with the rest of your money. As long as that ten percent fund is continuing to grow, you are practically guaranteed to have a significant nest egg waiting for you at retirement."

"But how much difference will a few hundred a month make?" Scott asked.

"Yeah, and isn't it just as good to start saving for retirement after you get the mortgage paid off and take care of the kids' education?" Rob seemed to be hoping as much as asking.

"That's what I thought," I said, "until I discovered the eighth wonder of the world."

"What's that, an honest politician?" Rob mused.

"No. Compound interest," I replied. "Given a little time, the magic of compound interest can turn even small amounts into significant sums. When I first started playing with some numbers on my computer, I was shocked — not because the numbers were big, but because the numbers were big and they had *my* name on them! I had seen financial tables and graphical projections before, but they were all hypothetical and didn't relate to me personally.

"Remember how I said one of the reasons we didn't start a ten percent plan last summer was because I didn't think that saving ten percent would amount to much? Well I figured it out. If Theresa and I invested $300 a month — *less* than ten percent of our net income — and earned twelve percent interest, how much do you think it would be worth thirty years later? I'll give you a hint. Three hundred a month times thirty years is a little over $100,000."

"I don't know, two . . . three hundred thousand," Rob guessed.

"Close," I teased, "over $1,000,000!"

"No way!" Scott shouted, loudly enough to turn the heads of the people at the next table. "You mean you can retire a millionaire, just by paying yourself ten percent?"

"It's hard to believe, isn't it?" I replied. "Ten percent magic — it really is amazing how, **over time, compound interest magically turns even small regular investments into personal fortunes**."

Seeing Rob butt out another cigarette made me remember the cost-of-smoking numbers I had shared with Kim. "Probably the best example of the magic of compound interest is something that might interest you, Rob. What do you think it would cost for a fifteen-year-old to smoke one pack of cigarettes a day until age sixty-five — assuming, of course, they live that long?"

"Let's see," he said. "Smokes cost about three to three-fifty a pack . . ."

"Let's say three dollars," I suggested.

". . . times 365 days a year is . . .," Rob seemed determined to come close on this one.

"About eleven hundred a year," I helped again.

"Is it really that much?" Rob seemed surprised. "I never really added it up." A few seconds later, he resumed, "A thousand a year for fifty years is a fifty thousand. Ouch, that's a lot already. Plus interest, I'll say about two hundred thousand dollars."

"Try $5,800,000!" was my straight-faced reply. "You forgot that the cost of cigarettes goes up every year. The fifteen-year-old who decides to start smoking a pack a day is giving up a retirement fund of almost six million dollars! And that's assuming the saved money is invested at only ten percent, and that cigarettes go up only ten percent a year."

"No way!" exclaimed Scott in disbelief.

"I'm afraid so. That works out to over twelve dollars a cigarette!" I exclaimed, visualizing what it would be like to roll up a ten-dollar bill, light it on fire, and repeat that twenty-five times a day. "Even someone in their forties like Rob can end up with $270,000 by investing the cost of one pack a day over the next twenty-five years."

Still no response from Rob.

"I wonder how much you'd save by giving up drinking," Pierre pondered, as he held up his empty.

"It doesn't matter," Rob finally piped up. "Beer is a staple food and a crucial part of all four basic food groups!" Although there were definitely better examples to illustrate the point, Rob reminded us that there were some things that were more important than money.

"Speaking of making millions, Talbot, weren't you supposed to find out how to earn twenty-five percent interest guaranteed?" Pierre asked.

"Yeah, what's the scoop? Is it for real or just a gimmick like I thought?" Rob demanded.

"It's for real," I confirmed. "And some people can earn even higher returns guaranteed."

"How?"

"Well, for starters, think about credit cards for a minute. Most department store cards charge almost thirty percent interest. Wouldn't you be able to earn thirty percent interest by paying off the card and avoiding the interest charge?"

"Hmmm," Scott thought for a second. "I guess you would."

"But it's more than that, much more," I went on. "You see, you have to pay it with after-tax dollars, so it's an after-tax interest rate. Because of taxes, you would have to have a GIC that paid fifty percent interest to end up with thirty percent after taxes!"

"I'm paying interest on a department store card," Scott announced. "You're saying that I'd be just as far ahead to pay off the department store card as I would to get a fifty percent GIC?"

"That's right. But you're not the only one who has been missing an easy opportunity for a great return. For years, Theresa and I left more than a thousand dollar balance on our credit cards."

"I'm not going to tell you how much we owe on our cards!" Rob declared, rolling his eyes. "But there's not much we can do about it for a while."

"Any luck on the job search?" I asked.

"No, not yet," he replied. "I've made a lot of contacts, though. They all say my resume will be kept on file, but there's nothing promising yet. I've been picking up the odd job on weekends helping a buddy with some of his carpentry contracts, but that barely covers gas money. With only a few months of unemployment left, if I don't get something soon, we'll have to get help from the in-laws just to keep up with the house payments."

"Well, if you don't have the money to pay down your credit cards for a guaranteed thirty to fifty percent return, why not try to get a personal loan to pay off the expensive credit card debt?" I offered. "By refinancing the debt at a lower rate, you'll save the difference in interest rates."

"Will they let you do that?"

"Why not?" I shrugged. "Besides, the worst they can do is say no. But make sure you don't go out and run up your cards again or you'll be worse off than before, paying off two debts instead of one. Paying interest instead of earning it turns the power of compounding against you."

Without taking his eyes off the Leafs game, Pierre began, "You know, it really is amazing what compound interest can do to your money. And it's actually very simple to figure out how fast it will grow. Have you guys heard of the rule of seventy-two?"

"Yeah," Scott joked. "It says that if anybody shoots less than seventy-two on the golf course, the other guys have to pay for the next round of golf!"

"No, seriously," Pierre said. "You can figure out how fast your money compounds by dividing seventy-two by the annual interest rate. The result is the number of years it takes your money to double. For example, if you average a nine percent return a year, seventy-two divided by nine is eight, so your money would double every eight years."

"Or in my case, my money would double every twelve years, since I'm lucky to get six percent," Scott countered.

"Talbot, you should tell them the example you told me at work," Pierre prompted, "the one that shows the cost of waiting."

"Good idea," I agreed. "Like Rob, I thought our retirement fund would be bigger if we waited to start saving until after the mortgage was paid off, and we could afford to save more. So I figured it out.

"Let's say that Scott goes ahead and sets up a ten percent fund, but because he gets married, he is only able to put aside $1,000 a year for the next forty years. His total investment is $40,000, but the magic of compound interest earning twelve percent a year turns it into $750,000.

"I, on the other hand, decide to wait twenty years until the house is paid off before starting to save for our retirement. With the kids gone and the mortgage paid off, Theresa and I can afford to invest $2,000 a year for the next twenty years. We end up investing the same $40,000, but since we waited twenty years to start, we end up with less than $150,000.

"Even though Scott invested the same total amount, he ends up with $600,000 more simply because he started early. To catch up to Scott, who started with a small amount when he was young, we need to invest over $10,000 a year — ten times as much!

"The point is that **procrastination is an investor's biggest enemy**. As you are now aware, given time, even small regular deposits can grow to a nice-sized retirement fund — if you start now and let compounding work for you."

"But what about people who didn't start saving when they were young, like my parents?" Scott queried. "Does this mean they won't be able to accumulate much before retirement?"

"No, not at all," I explained. "Obviously, the best thing would have been to start saving when they were young, but you can't change history. But that only gives them more reason to start saving now, to make sure they don't miss out on any more compounding time.

"And because you generally have more to invest when you're older, you can still accumulate large sums very quickly — especially if you take advantage of what the speaker called The Great WealthBuilder's Tax Shelter."

◁ 11 ▷
RRSPs – The WealthBuilder's Tax Shelter

"Did the government come out with a new tax shelter?" Scott asked.

"No, it's not new," I reported. "It's been around for decades. Most people refer to it as an RRSP, a Registered Retirement Savings Plan."

"So why did you call it a WealthBuilder's Tax Shelter?"

"Because that's a better name for it," I reasoned. "The words 'registered' and 'savings' make the plan seem like something that is complicated and requires sacrifice. And unfortunately, because it contains the word 'retirement', many young people tend to ignore RRSPs until they're older. To prove it, of the four of us, who has an RRSP? I don't. Scott, do you have one?"

Scott shook his head. I looked at Rob.

"You know I don't," he scoffed.

"So Pierre's the only one."

"And from what I learned at the workshop," Pierre sighed, "I wasn't taking advantage of RRSPs as well as I could have."

"So what makes an RRSP better than other investments?" Rob inquired.

"How would you like to effortlessly take care of your retirement by paying yourself first, *and* get a forty percent tax refund for every contribution you made?"

"RRSPs do that?" Rob asked. **"You get a tax refund for making an RRSP contribution?"**

"Yep. Depending on your tax bracket, you can get a tax deduction of up to fifty percent of your contribution," I replied.

"No wonder they're so popular. I'd do anything to save taxes!" Scott gasped.

"Hey, look at that," Rob said, as the game headed into overtime. "The Leafs have a chance to pick up another point."

"You know, it's pretty sad when you have to cling to the hopes of your team tying a game to get a point," Scott scoffed, shaking his head.

Rob, the die-hard Leafs fan, offered no retort.

"Contributing to an RRSP does more than give you an immediate tax deduction," I resumed. "Its other major benefit is that the returns the RRSP generate are allowed to **compound tax-free** until you take the money out of the plan. That could mean decades of tax-free compounding, which makes a tremendous difference to the size of your retirement fund."

"The seminar speaker gave an example that makes it tough to ignore the tax-sheltering benefits of RRSPs," Pierre carried on, pausing for a moment to remember the details. "Let's say that I, for some strange reason, never learned about RRSPs and start investing $1,000 a year.

"Scott invests the same $1,000 a year in his pay-your-self-first fund. But because he was lucky enough to benefit from a little barroom wisdom, he invests his money in an RRSP and adds his tax refunds of $400 each year. We both average an eight percent return. Twenty-five years later I have $46,000, but Scott's RRSP is worth over $100,000. His retirement fund is worth more than twice as much as mine simply because he used an RRSP to shelter his investment from tax."

"RRSPs are one of the best tax shelters in the world," I took over. "Since we live in one of the most highly-taxed countries in the world, it only makes sense to take every opportunity to reduce taxes as much as possible, and there is no easier or better way to do it than with an RRSP. **Everyone that pays taxes should have an RRSP.**"

"I still can't believe the government gives you a tax deduction for taking care of your own retirement," Scott remarked. "I'm only used to them increasing my taxes, not helping me lower them! Do you know any other ways to reduce taxes?"

"Not yet," I admitted. "But the last time I was in the bookstore, I saw lots of books on how to cut taxes. I think I'll pick one up before tax returns are due at the end of April and see what can be done to save on income tax. The way we've benefited from learning a little about insurance, mortgages, spending, and RRSPs, there's bound to be a few things I'm not aware of that could save us some money on taxes. It shouldn't be hard since I don't know anything now — except, of course, that the government takes too much."

"I'm still a little unclear on RRSPs," a puzzled Scott interjected. "You said that you get a tax deduction for contributions you make to an RRSP. If that's the case, couldn't you contribute enough to totally eliminate the tax you have to pay?" He raised his eyebrows with optimism.

Pierre laughed, crushing Scott's hopes of achieving the enviable position of paying no income tax. "The government is generous to subsidize our retirement savings with tax deductions, but they're not stupid. There are limits to the amount you can contribute to your RRSP."

"It was just a thought," Scott grinned.

"And a good one too," Pierre complimented. "But the government wisely set up limits to prevent people like Scott from reducing their taxable income to zero.

"Your annual contribution limit is currently $13,500, or eighteen percent of your previous year's earned income, whichever is lower. From that figure, your contribution limit is reduced by something called a pension adjustment. Although the government is continually changing the rules, at some point in the future, the maximum dollar limit is supposed to increase with national wage increases."

"What's a *pension adjustment?*"

"Your pension adjustment, or PA, reflects how much money was contributed by both you and your employer towards your retirement. If you belong to a registered pension plan or deferred profit-sharing plan, your employer and possibly yourself, will have already made retirement contributions, so you will have a pension adjustment that reduces your RRSP contribution room. If you're self-employed like me," Pierre pointed out, "you don't have a company pension plan, so your PA is zero."

"But that means you can contribute more," Scott objected. "That doesn't seem fair."

"Actually, it is," Pierre argued. "The system allows people with similar incomes to contribute the same total amount towards their retirement, regardless of the pension plan that they may or may not have. If you don't have a pension plan, you need to, and should be allowed to, contribute more than someone who has a good pension."

"I don't know about you guys," I stated, getting up to go to the bar, "but right now, my thirst is telling me to invest in another drink."

As Phil poured, he remarked, "Hey, I overheard you guys talking about RRSPs."

"Yeah, Pierre and I went to a workshop the other day and learned some things I wish I had known and acted on years ago," I told him. "With a pay-yourself-first plan subsidized with tax deductions, and the tax-free compounding, retirement saving couldn't be much easier. I bet you hear a lot of people talking about investments and RRSPs this time of year."

"Yeah, I do," Phil confirmed. "The other day I heard that in an effort to reduce the national debt, the government is considering replacing our Canadian currency with Canadian Tire money."

"Oh, really?"

"Yeah, and when you think about it, it actually makes sense for two reasons. There's more Canadian Tire money than Canadian dollars and, even better than that, it's worth more, too!"

"Thanks for the update, Phil," I played along.

"Scott tells me you've been learning about a lot more than RRSPs. He says you showed him how to save five hundred dollars a year on his insurance."

"He just didn't need the insurance, that's all. I was making even bigger mistakes before I started to learn a few basics about managing money. Once you're aware of all of your options and have a basic understanding of what's best for you, it's easy to save hundreds or even thousands of dollars a year. And now I'm learning that a little investment knowledge can make the difference between a retirement fund that's a couple hundred thousand, and a couple million!"

"Maybe we could get together sometime when I'm off work and chat about some of this stuff," Phil proposed. "On a bartender's income, you've got to do everything you can."

"Sure Phil, anytime. But the way we've been tipping you over the years, shouldn't you already be able to retire soon?" I kidded.

"Very funny!"

Returning to the guys, I wasn't even seated before Scott greeted me. "Talbot, about those RRSPs. How much of a tax refund do you get? You said it depends on your income. How do you know what your tax bracket is?"

"The refund you get from any tax deduction depends on what your *marginal tax rate* is. Your marginal tax rate is the percentage of income tax that you pay on the last dollar you earn. Or, to put it in terms you're more interested in, it's the percentage you'll get back from any tax deduction.

"Although the actual rates vary slightly for each province, there are basically only **three tax brackets**. The tax brackets change at incomes of approximately $30,000 and $60,000. If you make less than $30,000, your marginal tax rate is about twenty-seven percent. If you earn between thirty and sixty thousand, your marginal tax rate is a little over forty percent. And if you earn more than about $60,000, you lose over fifty percent of your last dollar to income taxes."

"That's highway robbery!" Scott exclaimed. "No wonder my overtime cheques seem like they've been cut in half. So if I earned $35,000 last year, how much of a tax deduction will I get if I contribute to an RRSP?"

"That depends," I replied, "on how much you contribute. If you contribute $5,000, you will get back about forty percent of that, for a tax savings of $2,000. Any contributions after that produce a refund of only twenty-seven percent because the marginal tax rate drops at the $30,000 level."

"So, it definitely helps to **have a basic understanding of the marginal tax rates,** and how they affect your investments," Pierre added.

"The other RRSP rule that you should be aware of is that if for some reason you can't maximize your RRSP contribution, you are allowed to carry forward any unused RRSP contribution room at least seven years. What that means," I explained, "is that if your RRSP limit was six thousand this year, but you only contributed five thousand, you would later be allowed to contribute an extra thousand dollars, over and above your normal contribution limit."

"But didn't the speaker say that it made sense to **maximize your RRSP contribution every year, even if you have to borrow** to do it?" Pierre asked me.

"Yeah, he did," I confirmed. "He warned that you shouldn't rely on the carry-forward rule because if you can't come up with the money for your full contribution now, how are you going to find even more money next year?

"Even if you have to borrow to top up your RRSP to the limit, you will still come out ahead in the long run if you can repay the loan within a year or so. Remember that because of the twenty-seven to fifty percent tax savings, you can pay back a big chunk of your loan when you get your refund."

"The other thing that you give up if you don't contribute the maximum," Pierre noted, "is the years of tax-free growth."

"That's right. We know what procrastination can do to our retirement fund," I added. "The best thing we can do is get the money inside the RRSP compounding tax-free as soon as possible. And the easiest way to do that is to start a monthly pay-yourself-first plan, so that you don't have to come up with one large sum at the end of February."

"What about paying down the mortgage?" Rob asked. "My brother has been wondering whether it's better to pay down his mortgage or contribute to his RRSP."

"That's a good question. And it's also very relevant. Most of us have mortgages and all of us should be contributing to an RRSP." I hesitated, while preparing a reply. "I haven't thought about that. We know that paying down your mortgage results in a high guaranteed return, but we also know that the tax-free compounding of an RRSP can easily double or triple a retirement fund. I'll have to play with some numbers on my computer and get back to you."

"Talking about mortgages," Rob began, "Scott, did you find a house yet?"

"No, I haven't, and to be honest with you, it hasn't really been a big priority. I've been keeping my eyes open, and if you see a good deal, let me know. But I'm not in a hurry to buy. I don't have much of a down payment yet, and you certainly don't expect me to give up my week of golf in Florida when you guys are up here shovelling out driveways."

"No, of course not," I consoled. "If it wasn't for your off-season practising, you'd probably just be an average hacker like Rob and I, and we wouldn't want that."

"You golfers know that an RRSP is not all yours, right?" Pierre sighed. "When I started my RRSP years ago, a lot of people I talked to didn't understand that."

"What do you mean it's not all mine?" Rob demanded. "If I contribute a thousand dollars to my RRSP, who else would it belong to?"

"The government. You see, **an RRSP is simply a government-approved tax *deferral* plan**. It's like a tax-shielding umbrella that you can use to keep the tax man away from an investment until you say so. The point is, you still owe tax on all of that money when you withdraw it from the plan. And when you do withdraw your RRSP funds, the money is added to your income and taxed accordingly. If you cashed all of your RRSP funds in one year and that extra income pushed you into the highest tax bracket, you could lose half of your RRSP to Revenue Canada.

"But cashing in your RRSP isn't the only option for getting your money out," Pierre added. "You could roll your RRSP into an annuity or a RRIF, or any combination, just as long as the plan is wrapped up by the end of the year you turn sixty-nine."

"I know that a RRIF is a Registered Retirement Income Fund, which allows your funds to continue to compound tax-free," Rob stated, impressing the three of us, "but what's an annuity?"

"An annuity is simply a contract with a life insurance company where you exchange a sum of money for a series of smaller regular payments. It works sort of like a mortgage, except you get the payments instead of making them," Pierre explained. "You will probably want a RRIF though, because although you will have to withdraw at least a minimum amount each year, your funds will continue to grow tax-free until you take them out. This lets you minimize taxes while maintaining complete control over how your funds are invested."

Pierre stood up, apparently looking for something. "I hate to ask an obvious question, but . . . where are the washrooms?"

"You see that big sign over the door that says 'KEEP OUT'," Rob pointed. "Go right through there."

"Of course," he muttered, shaking his head as he left. "I should have known."

"But there are ways to get your money out of your RRSP and pay little, if any, tax," I claimed, attracting the full attention of Scott and Rob who looked down from the hockey game.

"What are you talking about?" Scott asked. "Pierre just said you have to pay tax on that money when you take it out of your RRSP."

"I'm sure that some people expect to pay less tax on their RRSP funds when they retire because they think they will be in a lower tax bracket," I acknowledged. "And for people in the middle and upper tax brackets who stop earning a salary when they retire, that may be possible — especially if they take advantage of spousal RRSPs properly."

"What are spousal RRSPs?"

"As I understand it," I began, "spousal RRSPs are one of the best remaining ways for income splitting. A spousal RRSP allows one spouse, even a spouse in a common-law relationship, to make a contribution in the name of the other spouse.

"For someone like Rob, spousal RRSPs are ideal. Once he is working again — which I'm sure will be soon — he can make an RRSP contribution and take the tax deduction from his income, saving them the most tax now. Since Lisa currently has no other retirement income, when she withdraws the RRSP, the income will be taxed in her name at a lower rate.

"Because many couples aren't in the same tax bracket now and most won't have perfectly balanced retirement incomes, **generally one of the spouses should be contributing to a spousal RRSP**. By having the person in the higher tax bracket make the contribution, they get the largest possible deduction now. And by making the contribution in the name of the person with the lower income when the RRSP is going to be withdrawn, they will pay the least tax later."

"That does sound good," Rob nodded. "So later when I'm working again and set up a 'pay-my-wife-first' plan using a spousal RRSP, we come out ahead when we make the contribution *and* when we make withdrawals."

"I'm a little confused," Scott announced. "After years of getting used to the government doing nothing but take my money, why are they being so generous with RRSPs? The tax deductions, tax-free compounding, income splitting — what gives?"

"I know it's tough to admit that the government is actually doing something that's *good* for us," I replied, "but it is really in their best interest to encourage us to take care of our own retirements. They know the Canada Pension Plan is in trouble and the fewer people that depend on it, the better."

"Well, they're certainly encouraging us the right way. There's nothing like a forty percent tax deduction to motivate you to save!" Scott added.

"I'm sure that's one of the biggest reasons RRSPs are so popular," I agreed. "But be aware that the government doesn't want people to use spousal RRSPs for short-term income splitting. Their intention is to encourage you to build a retirement fund for your spouse. If Rob makes a spousal contribution and Lisa withdraws the money within the next three years, it will be taxed in Rob's name, not Lisa's.

"I should also point out that you can make contributions to both your own and a spousal plan, as long as the total contribution doesn't exceed your limit. But no matter what type you set up, make sure you **name your spouse as the beneficiary** both on the investment and, more importantly, in your will. If you don't, your RRSP will be taxed at death instead of being allowed to continue to grow tax-free in your spouse's name."

"Are spousal plans the only way to pay less tax when you withdraw money from your RRSP?" Scott asked, as Pierre rejoined us.

"No, not at all," I replied. "The normal way to reduce the tax due on RRSP withdrawals is to simply **withdraw your funds slowly when your income is lower**. As pointed out, that can be at retirement, but RRSPs can also be used for short-term financial benefits as well. With a little planning, you could use The WealthBuilder's Tax Shelter to get a free vacation anywhere in the world — paid for by the government," I stated softly, attracting the attention of even the most loyal hockey fans.

"Are you saying there's a 'free vacation RRSP' plan where the government subsidizes your vacation instead of your retirement?" a hopeful Scott asked. If anyone would take advantage of such a plan, it was Scott.

"No, there's nothing called a 'free vacation RRSP', but with a little planning, it's easy to do," I explained. "Let's say that Scott likes to travel and —"

"Slight understatement!" Rob underscored.

". . . and planned to take a year off to see Europe, South America, wherever. Over the next few years, he builds up a $15,000 RRSP. Because he is in the middle tax bracket, he will get tax refunds for more than forty percent of that, saving $6,300 in taxes. If he cashes in the RRSP during his year off, and that is his only income, he will only pay about $2,300 in income tax. The difference between the tax that he would have paid and what he ends up paying is $4,000.

"Using his RRSP to defer some income from a high-tax year to one he knows will have less income, he saves thousands in income tax." Scott was now smiling as I continued. "Now, is $4,000 enough money to take a two-week trip anywhere in the world?"

"I spent two months in Europe on less than that!" Scott exclaimed, obviously pleased with the 'RRSP vacation plan'. "You know, it's inspiring to know how to get a free vacation, but somehow it seems even more satisfying to stick Revenue Canada with the tab. They've sure stuck it to me over the years!"

"But it doesn't make sense to take a year off and lose a year's income just to save a few thousand in taxes," Rob protested.

"No, of course not," I concurred. "But if you're going to do it anyway, it's certainly worth knowing how to get the government to pay for at least some of it. And even if you're not an extensive traveller like Scott, you can use this same approach in other more common situations, like when you go back to school, or start a family —"

"Or start a business," Pierre cut in. "That's what I did, even though I didn't plan it that way. When I started my business, I withdrew some of my RRSPs during the first couple of years when the business wasn't generating much income. It allowed me to keep eating while things were getting started. And, because the RRSP withdrawals were most of my income at the time, I paid very little tax."

"I never thought about that one," I said. "But a more common possibility for short-term RRSP planning is when someone stays home to raise a family. If we had known about these things earlier and Theresa had built up a $15,000 RRSP, she could have done even better than Scott and his vacation plan. Because you can earn about $6,500 before you owe any taxes, if she stayed home for a few years to raise the children, she could withdraw $6,500 worth of RRSPs every year totally tax-free.

"Another time that your income is lower and a short-term RRSP might make sense is when you're temporarily laid off or disabled and can't work. In fact, **one of the better non-traditional reasons to build up a sizable RRSP is to provide additional income security**. Once you've built up a nice RRSP, if your income is interrupted for whatever reason, you will still be able to sleep at night knowing that your mortgage payments are covered."

"Gee," said Rob wistfully. "It'd sure be nice to have one now."

"And if you ever did need to use your RRSP as an income insurance plan," I added, "your benefits would be partially subsidized by the government."

"That's a good point," Pierre added, "especially for small business owners like me. Not only are RRSPs critical to the entrepreneur who doesn't have a pension plan, but they can also provide an emergency buffer if there are years that the business struggles."

"These few examples should show that RRSPs can be used for much more than retirement planning," I summarized. "RRSPs are a multi-purpose tax shelter that can benefit everyone, even in the short term, or when you're young. But if you are going to use one of these short-term tax-sheltering ideas, it should be in addition to the pay-yourself-first-ten-percent plan. By far the most valuable use of RRSPs is to ensure your financial independence at retirement."

The bar suddenly erupted with commotion as the Leafs won the game in overtime. "I told you they would win," Rob claimed smugly, as if he had never doubted the outcome.

"Talbot, did that book say anything about self-directed RRSPs?" Pierre asked. "I heard they can make sense in some situations."

"They can," I replied. "There are a couple of obvious situations when a self-directed RRSP makes sense. The first is when you want to invest in something that requires a self-directed plan, like mortgages for example. The second is when your total annual RRSP trustee fees exceed about a hundred dollars."

"Will you two kindly speak in one of Canada's two official languages?" a confused Scott demanded.

"You know how we said that an RRSP is really just a tax-sheltering umbrella that you can put over most Canadian investments?" Pierre asked Scott.

"Yeah."

"Well, a self-directed RRSP is simply one large umbrella," Pierre continued, "one plan for all of your RRSP investments instead of several individual plans. You can get one from the banks or trust companies, or through one of the brokerage houses."

"What's this trustee fee about?" Rob inquired. "Is that like a special fee you have to pay if you don't trust the person handling your money?"

"No, the RRSP trustee fee covers the cost of registering the plan with Revenue Canada and the ongoing reporting that must be done," Pierre replied.

"But don't be put off by the term self-directed," I added. "Obviously, you make the final decision as to what your money is invested in, whether you have several RRSPs or a single self-directed plan. In many cases, you can achieve the same thing with several regular RRSP investments at different institutions. The self-directed plan just simplifies things by allowing you to do all of your transactions with one institution. This is certainly a convenience, especially if you have guaranteed investments in your RRSP."

"Why is that?"

"Because your financial planner or broker can automatically shop around for you to get the best rate when they come due. One of the things I learned when we were saving up for the house is that we could have done much better than having Canada Savings Bonds. Thanks to our planner, we learned that you can generally get cashable GICs that pay as much as one percent more than CSBs. Not only that, you can buy them any time of the year."

"I've got a few CSBs," Pierre said. "You're saying I could get the same guarantee, but with a better rate?"

"With even more flexibility," I confirmed. "You could cash your CSBs tomorrow — I mean Monday — and probably get a cashable GIC with a higher interest rate."

"But finish what you were saying before," Rob demanded. "Why set up a self-directed plan when your trustee fees exceed a hundred dollars?"

"Because, according to the book, you can set up a self-directed plan for about a hundred dollars," I answered. "And another money-saving tip, no matter what type of

RRSP you have. Don't let the RRSP trustee fee be paid from your funds. Always pay it with money outside the plan. That way you don't reduce your RRSP funds."

"So what are you going to invest your RRSP in?" Scott asked me. "With rates where they are now, do you think you're better off with a short- or long-term GIC?"

"I don't think we'll be investing in Guaranteed Investment Certificates," I said. "With retirement decades away, we're definitely looking at a long-term investment. We want to invest in something that gives us the best chance of producing the highest returns over the long run."

"What investment does that?"

"Mutual funds, **equity mutual funds**," I replied. "The speaker at the seminar said they were **best for most people's long-term investments**. But I haven't finished reading that section of the book yet and I wanted to get a second opinion on a few things before we set up our RRSPs."

"I've heard of mutual funds," Scott reflected. "The guys at work talk about them all the time, but I haven't paid that much attention to them. How do you know which one is right for you and how to pick one?"

"Those are some of the things I need to find out," I replied, as the lights were turned down, indicating that the bar was closing. "Well, it looks like it's time to go. I'll fill you in when I learn more. See you guys next week."

◁ 12 ▷
Mutual Funds for Everyone

After I read the section of the book on mutual funds and talked to a few referred financial planners, there were still a few details I wanted to clarify with Sue before setting up our RRSPs. With some investment questions of her own, Theresa decided to join us and take the opportunity to leave Derek with Kim for a few hours.

Sue agreed to meet at Kool's for a change. Like many who enter Kool's for the first time, she was a little wide-eyed trying to observe and interpret the many sights. After Theresa and Sue had been introduced, we settled at a quiet table in the corner.

"This is quite a place," Sue nodded approvingly. "Very interesting . . . I don't suppose you want to tell me why there's a pine-box coffin holding a wax statue of Elvis suspended over the bar?"

"We'll leave that one up to you," I replied coyly, "but you are up to date on your life insurance premiums, aren't you?"

"Don't listen to him," Theresa tried to apologize for me. "The food here has never killed anybody."

"Yeah, thanks to the hospital right up the street!"

"Is there anything safe to eat here?" Sue asked, attempting to be serious and select an appetizer. "I did notice the management's disclaimer saying that it can't be held responsible for the rotten food, lousy service, or deaf bartenders."

"It's all good food — seriously," Theresa assured. "We generally get the nachos and never finish them because there are so many."

"And the one-cent special . . . that can't be for real, is it? Is the management crazy or what?"

"Yeah, it's for real," I answered. "And it applies to anything on the menu, too! But you have to remember this is Kool's. It's not like normal specials. Everything is available for one cent — one cent *off* their regular prices."

"Ah! . . . of course, and they let *everyone* take advantage of this?" Her reply was definitely sarcastic. "We should order extra to take advantage of the savings!"

After ordering, Sue resumed, "Theresa, I'm glad you decided to come, but it doesn't surprise me."

"Why is that?"

"Because today, at least in my experience, it's often the woman who manages the household finances. And it's a good thing too, because women are smarter than men — at least when it comes to money. Women are more inclined to seek out professional help and take the time to do the necessary research. Many men think that because they read the business section of the daily paper, they know all about finances. Even then, it doesn't take people long to figure out they're really reading the sports, not the business section."

"I read both!" I protested mildly.

"Yeah, but which one do you read first?" Theresa probed, trying to reveal my true priority.

"No comment."

Feeling outnumbered, I decided to change the subject. Confident that I would win, I challenged Sue to a friendly wager. If I was right about what the next-best investment to paying down credit cards was, she would buy me a drink for a change. If I was wrong, I would buy as usual.

Sue liked the offer. "So you think you know what the second-best investment is, eh?"

"Yeah, and it was almost too easy to figure out," I replied. "I went to a financial seminar a few weeks ago and it was obvious. After paying down high-interest debts, the best investment to make is an RRSP. You immediately get a return of thirty to fifty percent of your investment from the tax deduction, and all of the money gets to compound tax-free until you take it out. When I explained the benefits to some of my buddies, one of them couldn't believe that the government was responsible for something so good!"

Sue smiled contentedly, satisfied that her student had succeeded. "Very good. I guess I'm buying the next round," she graciously conceded, her tone indicating that she had expected to lose the bet.

"You knew I would figure it out!" I said, disappointed to know that my next beer was really a gift and not the result of winning an honest wager. "With all of the RRSP promotion in February, it's tough not to be aware of their benefits."

"I did expect you to figure it out," she admitted. "But don't belittle the discovery just because RRSPs receive a lot of attention this time of year. You'd be surprised how many people, even today, still don't know how powerful RRSPs can be for reducing taxes and increasing retirement savings. Even many of those that are aware still haven't gotten around to starting one."

"Well, Talbot and I are going to start one this week," Theresa interjected. "We just wanted to clarify a few details first to make sure we're making the right investment. What's the best way to invest your RRSP?"

"That's a good and often misunderstood question," Sue replied. "First, let's make sure we all understand some basics. Fundamentally, there are two ways to invest. You can either be an owner and invest directly in things that you expect to go up in value or you can be a loaner and lend it to someone who will pay you interest.

"Most of us in Canada are very familiar with the second option, being a loaner. We take our money to the bank and put it into a savings account, a GIC, a term deposit, or whatever. Then what does the bank do with your money?" she prompted.

"They lend it out."

"To whom?"

"To individuals and businesses, whoever needs money."

"Right. That's how the bank makes its money. They pay you eight percent interest on a GIC and then charge ten percent to take out a mortgage. The difference is their profit. So if you wanted a better return than GICs, what would you do?" Sue coaxed.

"You'd do what the bank does," I reasoned. "You'd invest in what they do."

"But the return on a mortgage isn't *guaranteed*," Theresa pointed out.

"Ah," Sue sighed, "the need for a guarantee. I'm going to leave that one for a minute. We'll talk about guarantees and real risk a little later. You said that banks also lend money out to businesses. Now if a business was willing to pay, say, ten percent interest to borrow money, they obviously expect to earn a higher return than that, since they are also in business to earn a profit."

"So you're saying we could get a better return by lending money directly to businesses?" Theresa questioned.

"Almost. I'm saying that you could get a better return by being a part of the business. By buying shares or stock of a company, you own a small piece of it. That way, when the business makes money, you get a share of the profits."

"But businesses can lose money and some even go bankrupt," I quickly pointed out, not excited about the prospect of sharing in their losses.

"That's true. Not all businesses make money and some do go bankrupt," she acknowledged. "Any single company can have a bad year or even disappear. That's why I don't recommend buying individual common stocks. If you put your money into two or three stocks and one of them goes bust, you're in trouble. Most people don't have enough money to properly diversify to protect against the inevitable bad stock.

"It's also very difficult to be successful at picking stocks. Only a few professional investment managers are successful at outperforming the market, and they've had years of training in business, economics, and investing. Even if you had the knowledge and discipline, do you have the time and money to do the constant research needed to locate good values, and to know when you've made a mistake and it's time to bail out?"

"I'd rather be spending my time with my family or on the golf course than watching our investments all the time," I admitted.

"And so would most people," Sue concurred. "On average, in the long run, corporations have to earn a higher return than the rate they borrow at, or they would go out of business. If there were no businesses, there would be no jobs and the whole economic system would collapse. That's not going to happen. So, in the long run, by investing directly in businesses and owning a part of them, you will achieve a higher return than being a loaner and lending your money by buying bonds or GICs. **Being an owner has to outperform being a loaner**. Does that make sense?"

"Yes," we agreed in unison.

Sue paused, reading our faces to make sure we understood before continuing. Theresa started before she had a chance. "Isn't investing in real estate another way to be an owner and get higher returns?"

"Yes, but real estate isn't an investment that can be tax-sheltered inside your RRSP, though it has been an excellent investment in the past. In the eighties, the baby boomers' demand for homes caused property values in some areas to make owners wealthy in a few years. It's also been said that over ninety percent of all millionaires have built their fortunes in real estate."

"Is that what you did? Do you own much real estate?"

"No. I do own a nice house on the river," she asserted. "But that's it. I never wanted the hassle of being a landlord. Real estate is one investment that can definitely take a lot of time — time I preferred to spend travelling. Unless you like being a bill collector and dealing with maintenance emergencies in the middle of the night, there are easier ways to invest your money.

"Don't misunderstand me. Real estate can still be very profitable. I just wouldn't count on the high returns of the eighties. With most of the baby boomers already owning homes, there are fewer new buyers. And you know what happens to prices when demand falls off."

"Yeah, prices drop," I said, recalling my high school economics course.

"There's another reason to invest for ownership, apart from the fact that it should give you the highest returns in the long run," Sue continued.

"What's that?"

"Taxes," she replied. "You see the government realizes how important businesses are to our economic prosperity, so they give you an incentive to invest in corporations. The money you earn from investing in Canadian corporations is taxed at a lower rate than interest-paying investments — in some cases, much lower.

"Isn't there one type of investment where you could earn $100,000 and not pay any tax?" Theresa asked.

"That used to be true," Sue started to explain. "Unfortunately, the government eliminated that opportunity in 1994. However, there are still good reasons to be involved with this type of investment, as I'll explain. But first, we should cover some basics.

"Investments can earn money in one of three ways and each is taxed differently. Investments can earn interest, dividends, or capital gains. Interest income, like from savings accounts and GICs, is taxed at your full marginal tax rate, much more than dividends or capital gains.

"Dividends are the distribution of a company's profits to the stockholders. Because you can claim a tax credit for dividend income from Canadian corporations, dividends are only taxed at about two-thirds of your normal tax rate. That means that earning eight percent in dividend income is the same as earning ten percent interest. Remember, all that matters to you is what your after-tax return is — how much you keep, not the before-tax return.

"The final type of investment income is capital gains. When you sell something, like a stock or real estate for example, for more than you paid for it, you have a capital gain. This is how you used to be able to earn $100,000 tax free, with the lifetime capital gains exemption."

"But don't you only have to pay tax on three-quarters of your capital gains?" I asked, to confirm a point I had learned at the seminar.

"That's true," Sue said. "There is still a twenty-five percent tax incentive to invest for capital gains. Another benefit is that you don't have to pay tax on capital gains every year, like you do for interest or dividend income.

You only have to pay tax when you actually sell your investment, which could be decades later."

"But none of these tax issues affect your RRSP investments, do they?" an unsure Theresa asked.

"That's right," Sue confirmed. "All investment earnings, no matter what type, are treated the same within an RRSP. Accumulations compound tax-free until you withdraw money from the plan. Then, the withdrawals are added to your income and taxed accordingly."

"So if buying individual stocks is too difficult and dangerously poor diversification, and real estate isn't eligible to be inside an RRSP, how do you invest for higher long-term returns?" I was confused by her conflicting message. "What about mutual funds? Aren't mutual funds a way to achieve the higher returns of ownership, while at the same time being diversified and eligible for your RRSP?"

"Mutual funds are the answer," Sue conceded, "and not just for your retirement investment needs. With the —"

"The speaker at the workshop said that equity mutual funds, those that invest in the stock market, are the best way to invest your RRSP funds," I butted in. "Is that true?"

"Generally, yes," she replied. "I'll clarify that in a minute. First, I want to point out that mutual funds mean more than equity investments. With the many different types of funds available, there is a mutual fund for practically every investment objective, whether you're saving for a vacation eight months from now or retirement decades down the road.

"As you probably already know, the concept of mutual funds is very simple. Many investors pool their money together and a professional money manager invests it according to well-established objectives. Some funds, like bond or mortgage funds, provide a regular, steady income, while others, like equity funds, provide little or no income and instead focus on achieving above-average long-term growth.

"**Money market funds** are another type of fund that you should be aware of. Because they invest primarily in government treasury bills, they are a guaranteed way to **get higher returns than bank accounts**. This makes them a better choice than savings accounts for excess cash because you can generally get them without any fees from the same place — your local bank or trust company, or wherever mutual funds are sold for that matter."

"But with a savings account, we can get at our money whenever we want," Theresa commented, not that we had a lot of cash weighting down the local bank.

"And you still can with mutual funds," Sue told her. "One of the overlooked benefits of most mutual funds is that they are very liquid, meaning you can generally cash in or transfer your funds in a few days.

"Do these things work?" Sue asked, pointing to the miniature *Rock-ola* juke box mounted on the wall at each table.

Never having had the desire to interrupt the Motown music that completed the bar's Detroit Tigers feeling, I didn't know. "Let's drop a quarter in and find out."

It surprised us all to hear the music change to one of the popular classics of the sixties.

"I hope you don't mind," she said, as she flipped through the box's selection of hits from the Beatles era. "These are the songs that were around when I was your age."

"No, go ahead."

"Another thing that some people don't realize," Sue continued, "is that anyone can take advantage of mutual funds. Since many fund investments can be started with as little as fifty dollars a month, mutual funds are for everyone, not just the rich. They're a way to become rich."

"Isn't diversification one of the biggest benefits of mutual funds?" I added.

"Yes, particularly for equity funds which tend to fluctuate more than the other types. Remember that lack of diversification is the major reason I don't recommend buying individual stocks as the way to achieve the benefits of ownership. But by investing in dozens of different companies, often in different industries, mutual funds solve that problem."

"But isn't investing in the stock market, even using diversified mutual funds, still risky?" Theresa asked. "Everyone remembers the market crash of October, '87."

"All mutual funds, especially equity funds, fluctuate in value. When investing in equity funds, there will be tough times, but you have to remember that the stock market has historically outperformed other investments *in the long run.*

"And they aren't guaranteed — their value goes up and down and some people consider this to be their biggest problem. But, as I'll explain shortly, this so-called 'problem' can be turned into your advantage — if you know how. And if you'll be patient, I'll discuss some truths about 'guarantees' and 'risk', the two words that influence investors' decisions more than any others.

"First, let me point out that a stock market crash, like the one in 1987, is much less likely to occur now, at least to the same degree. Since then, safeguards have been put in place to help prevent the market from going into free fall. If prices drop too much too quickly, trading is halted to give everyone a chance to think things through instead of reacting out of panic.

"My second point is that because stock market fluctuations are inevitable and for the most part unpredictable, this emphasizes the fact that equity funds are not suitable as short-term investments. Remember that equity funds should provide the best returns *in the long run,* over periods of seven to ten years or more."

"How do you turn the fact that mutual funds can go down in value into an advantage?" I asked, intrigued by the apparent contradiction.

"Simple," came the frank reply, "using **dollar cost averaging**. By investing the same amount at regular intervals into something that fluctuates in value, you **automatically buy more shares when the price drops, and fewer shares when prices rise**.

"Let me give you a simple example. If you start investing $200 a month into a fund when the price is twenty dollars a unit, you obviously end up with ten units. Now if the market suddenly dives and the price drops to ten dollars, what happens?"

"I shoot my investment broker!"

"No, seriously."

"You end up with twenty units," Theresa co-operated.

"That's right. Because you invested the same amount every month, you couldn't help but buy more shares when the price fell. You now have a total of thirty units, ten from the first month and twenty from the second month. But how many total units would you have if the price had stayed at twenty?"

"Let's see," I answered. "Ten the first month, and another ten the second month for a total of twenty units."

"So you end up with an *additional* ten units when the market falls," Sue noted.

"So you're saying that by investing the same amount every month, we actually *benefit* when the market drops?" Theresa asked.

"That's right. So the next time the market struggles, instead of wanting to shoot your broker, you should send her a thank-you!

"Frankly," Sue concluded, "putting away a regular amount into equity mutual funds every month is the near-perfect investment for retirement needs. You combine the benefits of dollar cost averaging with diversified, professionally-managed ownership for superior long-term returns. Because the plan doesn't require any expert knowledge or time on your part, you can simply forget about it and spend your free time enjoying life — instead of serving life for killing your broker!

"Your money goes to work for you as soon as it is available, instead of sitting idle in a bank account where you are tempted to spend it. And because a little comes off each paycheque, you don't even notice — until you wake up one day and discover you can retire in style."

"That makes perfect sense to me," I said, thinking we had found the ideal way to invest our pay-yourself-first fund, "but I was reading somewhere that it was best to keep only guaranteed investments inside your RRSP, since retirement funds should be invested conservatively and shouldn't involve any risks."

"Some of the so-called experts do recommend only 'guaranteed' products for your RRSP," Sue responded, "but you decide in a minute whether that makes sense. Another reason some people incorrectly recommend guaranteed investments for RRSPs is that the tax benefits of capital gains are lost if you put equities inside your RRSP. In light of what you now know, let's think about risk and guarantees for a minute and apply a little common sense. What I'm about to tell you is very important, so listen carefully.

"Many Canadians are quick to point out they are conservative investors who prefer to avoid risk, and for that reason they tend to stay away from equity investments that may go down in value in the short term. As I have emphasized, equities *are* too risky to be used for short-term investments. But true risk can only be evaluated in terms of the length of your investment.

"If you are investing for a two- or three-year time horizon or less, say to save up for a house or a vacation, then it doesn't make sense to invest in something that could drop in value before you need the money. But as your investment time horizon gets longer, as in the case of retirement savings, the concept of risk changes.

"There are a couple of facts about investment performances that should clarify what the real risk is when making a long-term investment. Two business professors at the university compared the returns for various types of Canadian investments over the thirty-seven-year period from 1950 to the end of 1987 — *after* the stock market crash. During that period, government-guaranteed investments averaged a return of between 5.2 and 6.2 percent. Investments in the Toronto stock market grew at a rate of 11.1 percent, almost five percent a year more.

"To put that difference in terms you can relate to, let's say it was 1950 and you had $1,000 to invest. If you chose guaranteed investments, thirty-seven years later you would have a little more than $9,000. If you chose the stock market, you would have over $49,000 — more than *five times as much* as choosing 'guaranteed' investments.

"Do you want to end up with a one-million-dollar retirement fund instead of five million, just so your investment never takes a temporary drop in value?"

"Of course not," stated Theresa.

"It seems like **investments that provide guarantees practically guarantee that, in the long term, you**

will end up with much less than you could have had," I added, ". . . in this case one-fifth as much."

"That's true. For a long-term investment, you shouldn't be concerned with the annual return from one year to the next, just the *average* annual return over the length of the investment. Even averaging just three percent more per year over thirty years can more than double your retirement funds! While most people who don't understand risk can't stand the possibility of their investments temporarily dropping in value by ten percent, they are quite content to slowly lose fifty percent of what they could have had . . . a little at a time, through years of lower returns.

"**To truly minimize risk,**" Sue summarized, "you need to **match the type of investment with length of the investment**. For short-term investments, definitely stick with cashable, guaranteed products. But for long-term investments that are more than ten years away, equity-type investments will generally give you the best returns with the lowest *total* risk — with the least chance of ending up with less than you could have."

"What about the fact that you lose the tax benefits of capital gains on your equity funds if you shelter them inside your RRSP?" I asked, referring to her earlier point. "Outside of an RRSP, you only pay tax on three-quarters of your capital gains."

"That's straightforward," Theresa claimed. "All investment income, no matter what type, compounds tax-free inside an RRSP, and it's all taxed the same way when you cash in. That makes choosing the type of RRSP investment even simpler than choosing non-sheltered investments where taxes make such a huge difference. Inside your RRSP, you simply want the investment that you expect to produce the best long-term returns — period."

"Very well said," said Sue. "I'm impressed. And if guaranteed investments historically produced the highest returns, you would want them in your RRSP, but they don't. Now if someone had both interest-bearing investments and equity-type investments, which investment should be sheltered inside the RRSP?" Sue tested.

"I know the answer to that one," I replied confidently. **"RRSPs should shelter the most highly-taxed investments that you have** so you save the most tax. Since interest income is taxed much more than dividends or capital gains, if you have any interest-bearing investments, they should be inside your RRSP."

"Good, you do understand," Sue affirmed. "I should also mention that for the person who isn't totally comfortable putting all of their long-term investments into equities, balanced mutual funds might offer a nice compromise. These funds invest in a combination of both stocks and bonds, and therefore tend to fluctuate less than pure equity funds. You still benefit from long-term ownership and, at the same time, you won't miss out on years when bond investments give the best returns."

"I'm glad you mentioned that," Theresa said. "Suddenly switching to equities might require too much of a leap of faith for someone who has always invested only in GICs or Canada Savings Bonds. Balanced funds sound like an excellent way to get started in mutual funds without being concerned about big fluctuations."

"Many of my clients have done exactly that," Sue recalled. "Later, after they have some personal experience with how mutual funds work for them, they either switch to equities, or keep their balanced funds and add separate equity funds."

"Sue, I'm sure that what you've already told us will add hundreds of thousands of dollars to our retirement funds, and you know we appreciate it, but aside from using dollar cost averaging to invest our RRSPs in equities to maximize long-term growth, what else can we do to further increase our returns — without involving risk or taking too much time?" My question wasn't motivated by greed as much as wanting to do our best with what we had. "You said that improving annual returns by only three percent could more than double a retirement fund."

◄ 13 ►
Easy Ways to Increase Investment Returns

Sue thought for a few seconds, tapping her decades of experience, before replying. "If someone were to offer you ten thousand dollars to work for a few hours, would you take it?"

Her question took me by surprise. It was certainly the most ridiculous question I had ever been asked. "Of course, who wouldn't?"

"Millions of people," she replied slowly, her expressionless face conveying the profoundness of the response. "Everyday, millions of people turn down the opportunity to earn thousands of dollars an hour. . . . They don't realize it, of course."

"What do you mean?" Thesesa asked impatiently, eager to discover the truth behind Sue's claim.

"You said that what you have learned already should add hundreds of thousands to your retirement fund."

"Yes."

"How much time did it take to learn how to do that?"

I quickly added up the time spent at the seminar, reading the book, and now talking to Sue. "Five or six hours."

"If it was ten hours and your new knowledge only added $100,000 to your retirement, what hourly rate would that be?" Sue asked, conveniently simplifying the calculation for me.

Silence. Sue's point was made — crystal clear.

"Ten thousand dollars an hour!" I finally replied slowly, taking time to let the lesson sink in. In my wildest dreams, I had never imagined doing anything that could pay thousands of dollars an hour! Sue's point quantified the benefit of a little financial knowledge in a way that would not soon be forgotten — if ever.

"So if by spending **a few hours a year** to learn a little more, you **could add a few hundred thousand to your retirement fund**, would it be worth your time?" she asked, not waiting for the obvious answer. "Unless you already have more money than you need, spending a few hours to learn how to improve your financial situation will be the most profitable use of your time — ten or a hundred times more lucrative than any salary you may be earning. I just wanted to put some perspective on that issue of 'taking too much time'."

"Speaking of time," Theresa said. "I think I'm going to give Kim a call and see how Derek is doing."

When Theresa returned, she seemed a little anxious.

"How's Derek?" I asked.

"He *was* asleep," she said, "until the phone woke him up. Then he started crying and woke Rachel. Poor Kim! Do you think we should go?"

"No. By the time we got there, they would both be asleep again. And now that we know that our time spent in our favourite bar — where there are no babies crying — is worth thousands of dollars an hour, I'm not in such a hurry to leave. I've got lots of questions left," I replied, now looking at Sue. "So, what other ways are there to increase our investment returns?"

"It's really very simple," she replied flatly. "Buy low and sell high."

Since I'd heard the expression dozens of times, Sue's advice was less than impressive. "Everyone knows that."

"Of course they know they *should* do it, but the problem is people don't know *how* to do it. To buy low requires that you buy when everyone else is selling, when the market is perceived as a bad place to invest."

"But you said that was difficult to do, even for professional money managers," Theresa countered.

"Yes, having an eye for value is difficult and requires a lot of self-confidence and discipline. But in at least one respect, you actually have an advantage over the professional fund manager. By buying a good mutual fund, you don't have to worry about your investment going bankrupt, because it's diversified. Knowing that your fund

will always rebound from bad years allows you to confidently buy additional units when your fund is low."

"But precisely how do you know when a fund is low?"

"First of all, you have to realize that 'low' and 'high' are
relative terms. They only have meaning when compared
to something else. Secondly, you can forget right now
about trying to hit the market highs or lows. No one, and
I mean no one, knows exactly when the market has
peaked or hit bottom. But you don't have to pick the
exact bottom to increase your returns.

"Let's assume that the long-term average annual
return for equity mutual funds is twelve percent. How
can that help you determine when to 'buy low' and 'sell
high'? Think about it for a minute. If the long-term average is twelve percent, then after any period that has an
annual return of less than twelve percent, wouldn't the
fund be considered 'low'?"

"I guess so," offered Theresa.

"For example, if the last year's annual return is negative ten percent, then doesn't it stand to reason that the
returns in the near future have a good probability of
being positive? In fact, sooner or later, the short-term
returns must actually be *higher* than the long-term average to make up for the lost ground during the bad year.

"On the other hand, if there is a time when your fund
has an annual return that is really high, isn't it only real-
istic to expect that sometime in the near future, the
short-term returns will be negative, or at the very least
below the long-term average?"

Sue again paused to assess our comprehension, and
then resumed. "I should point out, however, that **for a
long-term investment, it is more important to buy
low and continue to hold, than it is to sell high**. You
may not want to bother trying to 'sell high' at all. Studies
have shown that most of the total stock market gains
have occurred in a few very brief periods of time.

"If you sell after one year to take a twenty-five percent
gain and the market keeps climbing for the next two
years, you have missed out on the long-term benefits of
ownership that you were after in the first place. And it's
much more difficult to determine when a price is near its

peak and it's time to sell, than when it's 'on sale' and a good buy."

"I like that analogy," Theresa complimented, "where buying low is really the same as taking advantage of a sale."

"It's true," Sue went on. "And that's the right way to look at it. People will drive across town to save fifty dollars on a dress or suit that's on sale, but when investments are priced low, they hesitate. They don't realize that buying their investments on sale is the same thing, except of course they would benefit much more. One year when the market was down ten percent, I considered putting out a big sign saying: 'SALE: MUTUAL FUNDS 10% OFF!'

"Don't get me wrong. Dollar cost averaging is still the easiest way to automatically 'buy more low, and buy less high'. But you can enhance your returns slightly by applying a little common sense and understanding the fact that short-term returns have to average out to the long-term average.

"For example, when your neighbours and co-workers come to you and tell you how they have been making twenty and thirty percent returns in the market over the last few years, should you rush out and buy some equities to join the party?"

"No, because above-average returns can't continue forever," Theresa replied. "They must eventually fall to average out."

"And when they do fall, that's the time to buy their shares!" I added.

"A much better strategy," Sue assured with a grin, "not to mention very neighbourly! So don't be a rearview mirror investor and simply look to the investments that have done really well over the last year or two. That's an almost sure-fire way to reduce your returns because by the time most people get in, it's generally time to be getting out. And worse than the probable short-term disappointment, you might get discouraged and give up on mutual funds and their potential for better long-term returns."

"How do you keep on top of how your fund is doing, so you know when to buy on sale?" inquired Theresa.

"Your local newspaper's business section probably tracks the popular mutual funds. If you want more detail, *The Financial Post* and the *Globe and Mail* each produce excellent reviews of mutual fund performances on a monthly and quarterly basis that also include valuable investment related articles."

"Are there other ways we can increase returns?" I asked, noticing that her wine glass was nearly empty. I didn't want our ten-thousand-dollar-an-hour lesson to end because Sue's glass had run dry.

"Plenty," she replied. "We've just touched the surface. You sure you want it all now?"

"If you've got time," I replied. "I would rather know how to get the best returns possible before we set up our RRSPs than after. And we still haven't talked about how to pick a mutual fund."

"All right. First, a few more ways to increase returns — without taking a lot of time or risk," she winked.

"If you're using equity funds inside your RRSP, as I suggest you do, you can also improve returns slightly by making **maximum use of the foreign content limits**. Since American and international equity funds tend to outperform their Canadian counterparts by as much as three to five percent, you should get as much money as possible invested outside of Canada. You can have up to twenty percent of the book value of your RRSP invested outside of Canada. You also —"

"Excuse me, Sue," Theresa interrupted politely. "What's the book value?"

"Sorry, the book value is the amount that you contributed to the plan, as opposed to the current, higher value of the fund.

"Another thing you should do, that just takes a second when you are setting up your investment, is to **automatically reinvest the fund's dividends** to purchase additional units. With an equity fund, these dividends will be small, but compounded tax-free over the years, they can really add up.

"There's something else I didn't recommend to many clients, but since you asked, I might as well tell you," Sue added. "The classic way to increase returns is by using OPM."

"What's OPM, another TLA?"

"What's a TLA?" Sue replied, now able to relate to my lack of comprehension.

"It's my own term for Three Letter Acronym," I explained. "I use it whenever someone uses an acronym I'm not familiar with. It allows me to politely find out what people are talking about without feeling dumb. Now that I've told you mine, what does OPM stand for?"

"It's similar to my favourite beer, OP: Other People's. OPM stands for Other People's Money. The basic concept is very simple. **By borrowing money to invest, your investment returns are magnified**, or leveraged. For example, an investment that normally returns twelve percent might be leveraged into a return of sixteen percent.

"And what happens if your investment loses money?" Theresa inquired, aware that Murphy's Laws also affect investors.

"Leverage magnifies returns, it doesn't make them better," Sue emphasized. "A bad investment that loses twelve percent might be leveraged into a loss of sixteen percent. That's why it's important to know what you're doing. But making money using leverage isn't as hard as most people think. Many are surprised to learn that you can profit by borrowing money at ten percent and getting a nine percent return."

I looked at Theresa to see that she was as puzzled as I was.

"Make that another one," I admitted. "I'm no Einstein, but paying ten to get nine doesn't add up to me. That sounds like the kind of logic that creates the federal deficits." Even knowing how leverage magnified real estate gains didn't help me understand this apparent paradox.

"But you're not accounting for the impact of taxes," Sue clarified. "Since the interest expense of borrowing to invest is generally tax deductible, the after-tax cost of borrowing is only six percent for someone in the middle tax bracket."

"Therefore any after-tax return of more than six percent is profitable," Theresa concluded.

"Right," said Sue. "And because you only pay tax on three-quarters of your capital gains, the after-tax return on a nine percent capital gain is slightly more than six percent."

"Meaning that if you take advantage of the tax laws, you can actually come out ahead paying ten percent and getting only nine percent," I said, seeing that we hadn't been comparing apples to apples.

"Leverage isn't quite as simple as that," Sue conceded. "There are other issues as well, but you get the idea. I just wanted to point out one of the ways the rich get richer. Let me add a few quick comments about leverage before moving on to the biggest way to increase your retirement funds.

"First, the interest paid when you borrow to contribute to your RRSP is not deductible, just the contribution is.

"Secondly, there are a lot of people that could take advantage of leveraged investment returns without even taking on any more debt. I've met many who owe five or ten thousand dollars on credit cards or personal loans, and at the same time have other investments.

"They would be much further ahead to do a simple debt swap. If they cash in some investments to pay off their debts, they get a twenty to thirty percent guaranteed return, as you know. And if they borrow the same amount back to replace their original investments, they create new tax deductions because the interest expense of borrowing is now deductible. And all of this is done without increasing their debt by a penny!

"If you do someday decide to magnify returns using OPM, **see a professional** to make sure you are up to date on all of the implications of leveraging, and to help you choose investments with positive returns.

"And the most important point: only do it with a small amount. That way if things don't work out . . ."

"We get the message," Theresa reassured with a nod, while glancing at her watch.

"Don't worry," I said, reading her thoughts. "Derek is probably asleep again by now."

"Yeah, you're probably right, and he's in good hands. But we should think about going soon. Sue, what's the other way to increase our retirement funds?"

"Probably the best and easiest way to increase your retirement funds — without lowering your standard of living at all — is to simply **increase your monthly pay-yourself-first fund every year** as your income increases.

"When you get a raise, ten percent of your net income also goes up. By increasing your investment plan the same percentage that your income increases, you don't change your standard of living at all. But the difference to your retirement savings will amaze you.

"If you invested $100 every month at ten percent interest for thirty-five years, you would have about $340,000. But simply by increasing the contribution by five percent each year, you would end up with over $560,000.

"You mean we can add more than $200,000 to our retirement fund simply by increasing our monthly contribution each year by five percent?" I gasped.

"Yes, . . . if you started investing only $100 a month," Sue confirmed. "But if you're automatically setting aside at least ten percent of your income, between the two of you, you will more likely be contributing closer to $500 a month. So you should gain five times as much or —"

"An extra million dollars!" Theresa blurted out, flabbergasted that one idea could be worth over a million dollars!

I smiled and shook my head slowly. Although we'd already gained thousands of dollars in less than a year, the benefits of a little financial knowledge now had a new perspective. When it comes to managing money, the difference between knowing how and not knowing how is truly mind-boggling.

"I know it's getting late," I pressed on, "but what about some specifics on how to pick a fund? There are hundreds of different funds. Where is the best place to get one?"

"And does it make sense to buy a no-load fund," Theresa added, "one that doesn't charge a sales commission, or —"

"Hold on there! One question at a time," Sue pleaded. "You can buy mutual funds from many sources. Financial planners, stockbrokers, investment brokers, banks, trust companies and even some insurance companies all offer mutual funds.

"When choosing a mutual fund, the first thing to decide is the type of fund that suits your investment objectives. Remember what I said about matching the type of investment to the length of the investment to minimize your long-term risk and maximize your total return. For an RRSP investment that won't be needed for decades, an equity fund would be the best type to choose."

"Or a balanced fund," I added, "for those who want more stable growth."

"Of course. Then you need to select those funds that you expect to do well in the future."

"Funds?" Theresa questioned. "I thought mutual funds were already diversified. Are you saying we should have more than one?"

"Even with mutual funds," replied Sue, "it doesn't make sense to put all of your eggs in one basket. And with two to four well-selected mutual funds, you don't have to worry about trying to predict which fund will be the best. It's also good for your peace of mind to know that your future isn't entirely in the hands of one fund manager."

I nodded. "So how do you tell a good fund from a poor one? And does it makes sense to get a no-load fund to save the cost of the sales commission?"

"There are some excellent no-load funds," she asserted. "But apply a little common sense when deciding whether or not to get a fund that charges a sales commission. Some of the best mutual funds can only be acquired by paying a commission. Remember, you are only concerned with what *your* return is, after taxes and commissions.

"If you are going to keep your investment for ten years or more — as you should for equity funds — paying a four percent sales charge works out to less than half-a-percent commission per year. Does it make sense to avoid a fund that averages two percent higher so you don't have to pay a half percent for commissions?"

"Of course not."

"The other reason you might want to deal with a full-service broker," she pointed out, "is for the advice that you wouldn't get with a no-load fund. To compete for your business and maintain their clients, financial planners have become very knowledgeable and can provide other services that you might benefit from. Aside from helping you pick the right investments for your needs and keeping you up to date, many offer advice on insurance, taxes, and general financial planning. For many people, this service alone might justify the commission.

"But no matter what way you go, always **find out what *all* the commissions and fees are** before you buy. Front-load commissions, where you pay when you purchase, are generally negotiable, based on the amount of your investment and the amount of service you need.

"Rear-load funds, where you pay a commission when you cash in, aren't negotiable. Rear loads have become really popular because if you hold the fund long enough — usually a minimum of five to nine years — you don't end up paying a commission at all.

"If you buy a rear-load fund, find out if the fee is a percentage of the original amount or the amount at redemption. Are there any annual fees for administration? For an RRSP, how much is the annual trustee fee?"

"That's a lot to remember!" I pleaded.

"Don't worry, your financial planner will help you sort it all out," Sue assured. "When you and your planner are selecting your funds, the most important factor to keep in mind is the fund manager. Who manages the fund and how long have they been there?

"Remember, when you buy a mutual fund, you are essentially hiring a professional to manage your money for you. The quality of the fund's management determines your future returns, and the quality of the management is reflected in the fund's long-term track record — the five-, ten-, and fifteen-year annual returns.

"And be careful to look at performances for more than one point in time, too. Because equity funds fluctuate, their annual returns change every day. See how well the fund has done in good times and bad. You want a fund whose manager has proven he or she can consistently produce above-average returns."

Aware that it was getting late and that Sue had already shared a wealth of information, I started tidying up to leave. "Sue, before we go, I have one last question. What is the most valuable piece of financial advice? Of all of your financial knowledge, what is the single most important thing that a person can do to take care of their financial future?"

"Without a doubt," she replied, "**paying yourself first is the most valuable thing you can do**. By setting up a monthly investment plan of **at least ten percent of your net income, and increasing it each year**, you will painlessly and automatically ensure your future financial independence.

"And if you invest your monthly ten percent fund into several equity-based RRSPs," Sue summarized, "in one simple step, you will automatically benefit from all of the cornerstones of financial planning: forced savings, tax refunds, tax-free compounding, diversification, liquidity, dollar cost averaging, and superior long-term returns through ownership!

"After a lifetime of watching how people behave, I have concluded that most people's actions are based on habits. *Not* saving ten percent is a habit, just the same as saving ten percent is a habit. But make this one strategy a habit for life, **investing consistently** and patiently letting time work for you, and **you are practically guaranteed to be wealthy some day** — even if you manage your everyday finances as poorly as the government."

"That's all we need to hear. I'm sorry we kept you so long," Theresa apologized.

"Yeah," I seconded. "You know we owe you — a lot!"

"Don't worry about it. Paying for tonight was more than enough. And I'm sure that someday you'll take the time to share some of this knowledge with someone else."

◁ 14 ▷
Saving for Junior's Education

"Darling, are we still having problems with that dryer?" I asked Theresa as I struggled to get my jeans on.

"No, not that I know of. Why?"

"My pants seem to have shrunk again. What are you doing to them?"

"Why do you assume there is a problem with the dryer? Have you stepped on the scales lately?" she countered, noting that some parts of me were 'maturing' faster than others. "Don't you find it curious that only *your* clothes keep shrinking?"

It had been a while since I'd checked my weight, maybe for a reason.

"You know that denying the truth won't change anything. There has been a little more of you to love lately. ... *You're* not pregnant, are you?" she teased. That's what I loved about Theresa — she always knew how to cheer me up.

Seeing that this conversation was exposing more truth than I could handle, I looked for an escape. "When is Kim coming over?"

"I think that's her now," Theresa replied, checking the driveway.

"Hi, Kim. How are you? Where's Rachel?" Theresa asked as she took her coat.

"She's at her grandmother's."

"Kim, do you think that I've put on weight?" I asked. "You can tell me the truth — if you have to."

Kim eyed me for a few seconds and then answered sincerely, "You look as slim as ever."

"Thank you," I smiled back, appreciating her comment. It was good to have old friends who could lie for you when needed. "What's the score between you and Scott? It's been six months now that you've been going out. Things must be getting pretty serious. The last time Scott was in a relationship that lasted this long was in the sixth grade."

"Scott is one of the nicest guys I've ever met," she said sincerely, "and he really loves kids too. Sometimes I think he comes over to see Rachel as much as to see me. . . . But there aren't any wedding bells in the future, if that's what you're getting at."

"We'll see. Theresa tells me you wanted to talk about RESPs."

"Kim also has some news that she wanted to tell you in person," Theresa indicated.

"What's that?"

"I quit smoking," Kim announced, "for good. I haven't had a cigarette since the day after you showed me the cost of smoking."

"Great! I'm glad to hear that," I said. "So the numbers helped?"

"Yeah, they helped, but I didn't do it for the money. I know that money won't buy happiness — although no money won't buy anything. I quit for Rachel, for two reasons.

"I looked at what I had to show for working the last five years and there was nothing. I think I've been a pretty good mother for her emotionally, but I also want to know I can take care of her financial needs as well. With the small savings in the bank, if I lost my job, within months we would be forced to move to a cheaper apartment, probably to a worse neighbourhood. And since my parents helped me through college, I want to be sure I can help Rachel as well, if she needs it.

"The more important reason I quit was to set a better example for her. Everyone knows what smoking does to your health, and I really couldn't expect her to not do something that I did everyday."

"Well, we're both happy for you, and Rachel," Theresa added warmly.

"I've been putting the money I saved by quitting into a separate account for Rachel's education," Kim went on, "and I wanted to ask you what's the best way to invest it.

Theresa says that you've learned a lot about finances in the last year and should be able to help."

"I've learned a few things," I replied, "and since having Derek, we've kind of been forced to look into education savings plans. For a few months after Derek was born, it seemed that every week another salesperson was calling to sell us an education plan or life insurance.

"After looking into RESPs — Registered Education Savings Plans — and some alternatives, we learned that providing for a child's education is very easy. You should be able to take care of Rachel's education using just a portion of the money you're saving by not smoking."

"So I should get an RESP?" Kim asked. "A couple of people tried to sell me one of those plans after Rachel was born, but at the time I was more concerned with paying for diapers than an education that was eighteen years away."

"RESPs are good in many ways," I explained. "They allow your funds to grow tax-free until the child goes on to post-secondary education. Then, when the money is taken out, it is taxed in the child's name instead of yours. Since they aren't likely to have much income, they should pay little, if any, tax."

"The tax benefits make the RESP sound pretty good," Kim noted. "Is that what you set up for Derek?"

"Yes, ... now", I replied. "But not initially."

"What do you mean?"

"Despite the advantages of RESPs, until recently they had one serious drawback that, for us, was too big a risk. When Derek was born, if he didn't go on to college or university, we would have lost all of the RESP's growth. We could get back all of the money that we contributed, but that's not much compared to the accumulated growth over almost two decades.

"So initially we chose a better option that didn't have the risk of losing the growth. Since the money you receive from the **Child Tax Benefit** belongs to Rachel, it can be **invested in her name**. When you set up the investment, the name should read 'Kim Reynolds *In*

Trust For Rachel'. That way, the money legally belongs to her and is taxed in her name, not yours."

"And because she doesn't earn any money, there isn't any tax to pay," Kim quickly concluded.

"Right, which means that you have virtually the same tax benefits as the RESP," I confirmed. "But you still have total control over the money — all of it. There is no risk that you will lose the accumulated growth if she doesn't go on to college."

"But what did you invest in, and how much should be enough?" Kim persisted.

"We started investing fifty dollars a month into an equity mutual fund using the informal trust setup," Theresa answered. "Talbot figured out that fifty dollars a month should grow to at least $25,000 after eighteen years. Even after inflation, that should cover a good portion of the cost of tuition and books. Personally, we don't believe that it's the parents' responsibility to finance the entire education. But we do want to know that if one of our kids doesn't earn enough to cover their own expenses, they won't have to delay their education for lack of money."

"Why an equity mutual fund?" Kim asked.

"A couple of reasons make a good **international equity fund the ideal education savings plan**," I replied. "The most important one is that it should pro-vide the best returns over the long run, and with college eighteen or more years away, you're definitely looking at a long-term investment.

"The other reason is that, unlike an RESP which limits the amount you can contribute each year, there are no restrictions on the amount you can invest in the child's name. If you wanted a larger education fund to pay for, say, Rachel's more expensive Harvard tuition, you or a relative could invest as much as you want in Rachel's name without the attribution rules affecting your tax-free growth."

"What are *attribution rules?*"

"Attribution rules are laws set up to discourage income splitting among family members. For example, if one spouse gives money to the other spouse and that money is invested, the investment income is attributed — or taxed back — to the donor.

"The attribution rule you are interested in is what happens when you give money to a child and it is invested. In this situation, only interest and dividend income is taxed back to the donor. Capital gains aren't. Since most of the growth in an equity fund is capital gains, using the simple 'In Trust For' approach, you still get the RESP's benefit of tax-free accumulation in the child's name, without the risk of forfeiting the growth if they don't go on to college."

"Recently, however," Theresa took over, "the government has significantly improved RESPs to really encourage parents to help save for their children's education.

"They have essentially eliminated the risk of losing the growth if a child doesn't go to school. Now, if the child doesn't use the money for education, you can transfer up to $50,000 of the growth to your RRSP, if you have enough contribution room. If you don't have enough room, you can still recover the RESP's growth after paying a 20% penalty on top of your normal tax rate. To further reduce the risk, you can set up a family plan where you can name several beneficiaries."

"But the biggest improvement to RESPs," I added in, "is that the **government gives you a 20% grant of up to $400 per year for saving in an RESP.** Annual RESP contributions of up to $2,000 are eligible for the grant, and if unused, the grant room can be carried forward. Our advisor explained some of the details to qualify for the grant, and how you must repay the grants if the child doesn't go on to school. But with the risk of losing the growth mostly eliminated, the 20% RESP grant is too good to pass up.

"One thing, though. If you do use an equity fund for your education plan, either using an 'In Trust For' approach, or inside an RESP like we are now, make sure you switch into GICs three or four years before Rachel will need the funds."

"Why not just leave it there until it's needed?"

"Because, while equity funds are an excellent long-term investment, their fluctuating values make them too risky in the short term. When you need your money in less than five years, that becomes a short-term investment. When that happens, you should try to pick a time when the stock market is high and move the money to something that offers short-term guarantees.

"For the same reason, you wouldn't want to leave your retirement funds in equities until the day before you need them. On the other hand, you wouldn't want to move all of your retirement money into guaranteed investments when you retire either, as several experts suggest. Since *some* of that retirement money won't be needed for another ten to twenty years, some of your funds should stay in equities until five years or so before you need the money."

"So fifty or sixty dollars a month should do it," Kim recapped. "By quitting smoking, I've been saving over a hundred dollars a month. That will leave me with money to spare!"

"What would you say if I told you there was a way to get the government to pay for most of the fifty dollars a month needed for Rachel's education?" I asked.

"I'd say let's do it!"

"Well, if you took that hundred dollars a month and put it into an RRSP for yourself, you would get a tax refund of about forty dollars a month. If you took the RRSP refund of almost $500 a year and put it into an RESP for Rachel, you would get an extra $100 a year from the free RESP grant.

"You end up starting an RRSP, which will eventually give you the financial buffer you need to feel secure, and Rachel gets much of her education paid for — all for no more money than you were spending six months ago!"

Kim was obviously pleased with the 'government-paid' education plan, and looked for a way to express her appreciation. "You know, Talbot, if I look closely, I think you may have actually *lost* weight lately!"

◁ 15 ▷
Reducing Taxes and
Minding My Own Business

"Pierre, what's going on? I thought you said this program was working," I asked my colleague, as we stared at my computer and wondered what to do next.

"I don't know. It worked fine at my place."

Even though I like all the wonderful things they can do for us, there are times when computers can frustrate anyone. "Pierre, do you know the difference between hardware and software?"

"No, what?"

"You can kick hardware! Let's leave it till Monday and see if we can get it working then."

"Did you ever get a chance to read that tax reduction book you got a while ago?" Pierre asked. "With tax returns due at the end of the month, I want to make sure I'm not missing anything that could save me some money. What else can I do to cut taxes, besides contributing to an RRSP?"

"Well, the most important thing I learned about taxes is how valuable it is just to be aware of the basics. Since there isn't that much a salaried person can do, it really didn't take long to make sure we weren't missing any tax credits or deductions. It was embarrassing the number of tax deductions we weren't taking advantage of. Even Revenue Canada's general tax guide — which is free — is a good source of tax tips, and it's easier to read than I thought.

"For instance, I didn't know that **moving expenses are deductible** whenever you move at least forty kilometres to start a new job, even if it's a summer job when you're in college or university. My last summer of college, I had a good job and ended up paying taxes, which would have been reduced had someone told me about this deduction."

"And I suppose if you move to set up a business, the expenses are deductible too?" Pierre wondered.

"Definitely, why?"

"I didn't deduct my moving expenses when I moved from Toronto two years ago."

"Did you sell a house when you moved?"

"Yeah, why?"

"Because all expenses related to the move are deductible, not just the moving van. Things like legal fees, land transfer taxes, and the biggest of all — real estate commissions."

"I sold a $250,000 house," Pierre said. "The commissions alone were almost $15,000. Are you telling me I missed a $15,000 deduction?"

"Which would have saved you about $7,000, based on your tax bracket," I added.

"You really know how to cheer a guy up," Pierre huffed. "I think I would feel better now if I *hadn't* learned that I passed up $7,000."

"It's not gone," I announced. "Under the government's new Fairness Program, **you can have any tax return** in the last seven years **reassessed**. That means that if you discover a missed credit, deduction or an error in any of those past returns, you can get it corrected and put hundreds or, in your case, thousands of dollars back in your pocket."

"You're kidding, right?" Pierre looked at me for his answer. "You're not kidding. Whew! I feel a lot better now."

"Some of the other **commonly missed tax deductions and credits** include medical costs if they are high enough, union or professional dues, alimony or maintenance payments, educational expenses, and child care expenses. And Theresa's best friend, who is a single mother, didn't know that she was entitled to the equivalent-to-married credit. Even the cost of safety-deposit boxes and home safes is deductible.

"I was also pleased to find out that investment counselling and portfolio management services are deductible," I reported. "That means that when I pay for a financial expert's advice, the real cost is forty percent less. I guess the government feels that if the counselling makes me a better investor, I will earn more money for them to tax."

"Talbot, you've already named too many deductions that I wasn't aware of, one of which could have cost me seven grand," Pierre said humbly. "Do you think I could borrow that book for a few days to make sure I understand the basics?"

"Sure, our tax returns are already done. Borrow it as long as you want."

"What are some of the other things in here that I should pay attention to?" Pierre asked.

"Well, it really pays to know what your marginal tax rate is and how different types of investments are taxed," I replied. "Since you are only concerned with how much of an investment you get to keep, you need to know what your after-tax returns are when comparing investment alternatives. That means knowing capital gains and dividend income are taxed much less than interest from investments like savings accounts and GICs. Also, no tax is due on capital gains until you actually sell the investment.

"Income splitting is another way that couples can reduce taxes, despite the government's efforts to discourage it. And, by the way, if you think you can simply move in with someone to avoid the commitments of marriage, be aware that common-law couples are now taxed the same as married couples."

"I'd rather not talk about income splitting," Pierre chuckled. "I found out the hard way that when you get divorced, alimony payments start splitting your income forever. Sometimes I think the word should be pronounced 'all-le-money'. You know, it's not easy trying to support an ex-wife and two divorce lawyers!"

"But knowing how to split income properly will benefit Theresa and I in a few years when she works part-time to be home with the kids more. By putting all of our savings accounts and other non-RRSP investments in her name, we'll save tax because her marginal tax rate will be lower when she drops to part-time."

"A spousal RRSP is also a good way to split income," Pierre added, "as long as you don't split it the way I did!"

"Pierre, there was one part of the book that talked about dozens of ways to reduce taxes that aren't available to most people — by starting your own business. You've run your own business as a consultant for years. What's involved in setting one up? Is all the paperwork worth the extra deductions?"

"Starting a sole proprietorship, where you are the only owner of the business, or a partnership, requires only filling out a registration form from the Ministry of Consumer and Commercial Relations and paying a small licensing fee," he replied. "The government obviously wants to encourage the creation of new businesses and helps you as much as it can with information, counselling, and even free grants. The province has a toll-free Business Start-Up Hotline. You can find it in the blue pages of the phone book, and it should help you get pointed in the right direction."

"Tell me more about these grants," I insisted. "Are you saying that the government gives you money to start a business?"

"Not exactly. There are government-assisted loan programs for those just starting up, but even better than that are the grants and incentive programs that are available to any business. To help boost employment, the **government** often gives out thousands of dollars in **grants** to help businesses hire staff or train them.

"If you're even considering starting a legitimate small business," he went on, "I would strongly recommend that you do, particularly a part-time one. There are all kinds of benefits: you get to be your own boss, reduce taxes, pick your own hours (all eighteen of them sometimes), and, of course, there's the potential to make a lot of money — if your clients pay. Seriously, if you can work on your own, running your own business is tough to beat."

"Why is it better to start a part-time business?"

"A **part-time business**, in addition to a full or part-time job, is an ideal setup for several reasons," he explained. "First of all, in terms of **tax benefits**, most business-related expenses can be deducted against your salaried income. A portion of things like your computer, office equipment, car expenses, and even a portion of any business-related meals and entertainment now become legal tax deductions."

"Isn't a portion of your total housing costs deductible if you have a home office?" I asked.

"Yes," Pierre confirmed. "As a 'homepreneur' — an entrepreneur working out of your home — you're entitled to additional deductions. If, for example, you use part of your home exclusively as your office, a portion of your mortgage interest or rent, heating, utilities, and maintenance can easily add up to thousands of dollars of deductions. But these expenses are only deductible against business income.

"Possibly the best reason to start a part-time business is for the **additional income security**. Most people sleep better knowing they're not totally dependent on their employer always having a job for them. If you ever did get laid off, the business lets you make ends meet until you either get another job or discover the business can support you on its own."

"I never thought about the security aspect," I reflected, "but you're right. No matter how bleak the job market looks, running your own business is the one job you never get turned down for. But you still have to come up with an idea for a product or service."

"Not any more," Pierre claimed. "There is a way that **anyone can start their own business** and make money almost immediately, even those who don't have a marketable skill or idea of their own."

"How?"

"**By joining one of the many network marketing companies**," Pierre replied. "You get the benefits of running your own independent business, without having to figure out what to sell and how to do it profitably. You don't need any special background and, unlike franchises, you can get started with almost no money."

"Are you talking about multi-level companies that sell soaps or cosmetics?"

"Some sell those types of things, but there are dozens of network marketing companies that sell all kinds of products and services. For many people, like my sister, who want to work casually during their spare time, finding a network marketing company with a product that you like is a good way to make a little supplemental income. She really likes the extra hundred dollars a month or so, and normally uses it as extra fun money for things like vacations — although she did use it to make her RRSP contribution last year."

"That's interesting," I said, "especially for those who already have sales skills. I wonder if Rob has looked into these possibilities."

"I don't know. We should ask him."

"But no matter what business you start, don't you have to show a profit within the first three years or risk losing all of your past tax deductions?"

"I heard that rumour too," Pierre said, shaking his head, "but it's not true. The definition distinguishing a hobby, where you cannot deduct expenses, from a business is that you must have a reasonable chance of making a profit — at some point in the future. It would be unrealistic for Revenue Canada to demand that you be profitable within a certain period of time, as long as you're legitimately trying to turn a profit. Let's face it, some of the largest and oldest corporations in the country have years where they lose money."

"That's true," I nodded. "You know, the idea of being a part-time homepreneur is sounding better all the time. If I'm going to spend extra time on the computer, I might as well be making money doing it, especially if it means thousands of dollars in additional tax deductions."

"You're mostly interested in microcomputers, aren't you?" asked Pierre.

"Yeah, why?"

"Because my business is strictly larger systems, like at the board of education, and often my clients ask for some development on microcomputers. Since I know that you do good work, I should be able to refer some business to you. Let me know when you have some business cards and we'll see what we can do."

"Thanks, Pierre. I'd appreciate that."

"When you do set up your business, you will have even more opportunities for income splitting," he added. "If Theresa is part-time, you could pay her a reasonable salary to help with the record keeping. That way, you move income from a higher tax bracket to a lower one.

"Another thing I did was to pay my kids a small amount to keep the office clean and run the odd errand. It was better than an allowance, since I got another deduction, and the kids learned the value of working for the money.

"Oh, one last thing. You'll need a good accountant. Because the tax laws are so complicated and the rules change so often, their unbiased expertise can save you a fortune."

"If you are aware of the basics so you know what to tell them," I added.

"Right, like moving expenses," Pierre agreed. "I'm going to make sure there isn't anything else that I should have told him." He fanned through the book as he headed out to the living room where Theresa was feeding Derek.

"Theresa, how do you like the idea of Talbot starting a part-time business for extra income and tax deductions?" Pierre asked.

"Sounds good," she replied, "as long as he keeps his full-time job and doesn't forget about his responsibilities around the house."

"Good, then it's unanimous," Pierre asserted, as he moved towards the door. "I'm running late. If you have any questions about getting started, give me a call."

"Thanks, Pierre, we'll see you tonight at the rink."

"Talbot, speaking of calls," Theresa began. "Rob called earlier with good news. He got a job! He didn't give a lot of details but he sounded pretty happy — and relieved."

"Yeah, I bet. It's been hard for them. I'm glad things have finally turned around."

"Oh, and he also mentioned something about RRSPs and paying down the mortgage. Does that ring a bell?"

"Oh yeah," I remembered, "his brother wanted to know which was better. I did some analysis before we made our RRSP contributions, but I guess I never told Rob about it. That's okay, I'll see him tonight and tell him then."

◁ 16 ▷

Everyone Can Free Up
Money to Invest

"Who won tonight?" Phil asked as we entered Kool's after our Saturday night hockey game.

"We did. The win moves us up to second in the league," Scott replied proudly, while signalling Phil to serve up the usual.

"Yeah," Rob laughed, "too bad it's second from the bottom!"

"He didn't have to know that!" Pierre scolded. "Do you want everyone to know that we're just out for a good time?"

"Hey, Talbot, how is junior doing? Are you and Theresa expecting another one yet?" Phil asked politely.

"Not yet," I replied. "But Derek is doing fine and getting bigger every day."

"Kids are wonderful," Rob added, "especially when they start talking. They certainly have a different view of the world. Like the other day I found out how I was aging when our three-year-old turned to me with a deeply concerned look and said, 'Daddy, I think you're drinking too much milk.' When I asked why, he replied: 'Because it's starting to come through in your hair!'

"And the youngest one's just started into her climbing phase. We've had to rescue her from the tops of tables, counters . . . she was even in the sink once. She never sits still . . . . reminds me of the Energizer bunny. She just keeps on going, and going, . . . and going . . . Sometimes I wish she *had* batteries so we could take them out!"

"Sounds like I've got a lot to look forward to," I grinned.

"So tell us more about your new job, Rob," Scott cut in. "Did you find something in sales like you wanted?"

"Yeah, actually things turned out pretty well. CJ's Office Warehouse down on Dundas Street needed a sales supervisor. They liked my experience as a manager at the furniture store and were impressed by my sales record. The store owner also explained that the current store manager is going to be transferred to set up another location and, depending on how the next few months go, I have a good chance of getting that job. It even pays more than I was making before!"

"So are you looking forward to getting back to work?" Pierre asked.

"You better believe it," he nodded. "It sure will be nice to have money coming in again. You really appreciate things after you've had them taken away for a while. Security was something I took for granted before. Now, I know it's *my* responsibility, not the government's or my employer's."

"Well, we're all glad to hear that things will soon be back to normal," Scott said, acting as our spokesman.

"Oh, Talbot, my brother called again the other day asking whether it was better to pay down his mortgage or contribute to an RRSP," Rob went on. "Did you ever look into that? Back in February, when we talked about it, you said you needed to do some calculations."

"Sorry about that, Rob," I apologized. "I meant to get back to you on that. It took some time to evaluate because it was an excellent question. On one hand, the RRSP offers a nice refund and tax-free compounding, while paying down a non-deductible debt, like the mortgage, results in a very high, guaranteed return."

"Don't some experts recommend that you do both by contributing to your RRSP, and then using the tax refund to pay down the mortgage?" Pierre noted.

"Yeah, they do," I replied, "and at first I felt that was the answer, until I thought about it for a minute. If it was better to put a thousand dollars into an RRSP, then why is it all of a sudden better to pay down the mortgage when the refund comes in? If the best place for the money was the RRSP initially, then surely the best place for the refund is back into the RRSP to generate another refund."

"And what about when mortgage rates are over fifteen percent?" Scott added. "You'd think that if mortgage rates are high enough, you would be better off paying down that expensive debt."

"I agree," I concurred. "So the question is, 'What interest rate is so high that paying down the debt is better than contributing to an RRSP?' Well, after evaluating numerous situations on the computer, I found that most people will be further ahead, mathematically at least, to **contribute to an RRSP unless their mortgage rate is at least three percent higher than their average RRSP return**.

"For example, if you expect that over the long run, your RRSP will average ten percent growth a year, then you should pay down any loan charging thirteen percent interest or more. That's when interest charges are high, and paying down the debt becomes the priority. Otherwise — which is most of the time — the RRSP is the way to go."

"Does that apply to all situations," Pierre inquired, "or just your own?"

"It totally depends on how much of your mortgage payment you start investing when the house is paid off," I said. "I presumed that you would invest two-thirds of your mortgage payments after the mortgage is gone. I don't know about you guys, but I can't honestly say that once our mortgage is gone and our expenses drop by over $10,000 a year, we're going to invest every penny of that extra money. I'm sure that some of it will become extra fun money for travelling more and rewarding ourselves for paying off the mortgage.

"If you're not going to invest any of that extra money, then the RRSP is definitely better, because eventually you will have a debt-free home *and* a nice RRSP. In this sense, contributing to the RRSP has the benefit of being an additional forced savings plan.

"On the other hand, someone like Pierre, who likes to invest as much as possible so he can be a millionaire when he's fifty, should pay down his mortgage first." The enterprising entrepreneur looked away modestly. "If he invests all of his mortgage payment after the mortgage is gone, he would be further ahead paying down the mortgage first, even if it was a couple percent less than his average RRSP return.

"But for most people, myself included, RRSPs should come ahead of paying down the mortgage," I summarized.

"Even so, Talbot, I still think I would feel better knowing that our mortgage is paid off. I mean, until it's paid off, there's still the risk that you could lose the house — everything — if you couldn't make the payments," the recently laid-off Rob reasoned.

"I felt the same way initially," I responded, "before I thought about which option really gives me more peace of mind. Remember when we talked about RRSPs and how they can provide income security? Which situation would make you feel more secure: owing $80,000 and having no emergency funds, or owing $100,000 and having $20,000 in RRSPs?

"Whether you owe eighty or a hundred thousand, it doesn't matter. If you stop making payments, you could lose the house. If your cheques stopped coming tomorrow, how many months could you continue to cover all of your expenses?"

"Don't you mean how many weeks?" Rob corrected.

"Many people, Theresa and I included, would be out of money in less than three months. Wouldn't you feel more secure knowing that between a $20,000 income security buffer and unemployment insurance, you have the next couple years of payments covered?"

"I never thought about it like that," Rob admitted.

"For many, this **peace of mind from the RRSP's extra security may be more important** than which option is mathematically better. Another thing to factor into the decision is the fact that the RRSP is much more liquid or easily cashed in than a house. If you needed cash to take care of an emergency or a once-in-a-lifetime opportunity, it's a lot easier to cash a few thousand out of the RRSP than trying to sell a part of your living room."

"That's why I'm going to start an RRSP," Rob announced confidently. "A few months after I'm settled into the new job, I'm going to set up a pay-yourself-first plan — or I guess that should be a pay-my-wife-first plan since a spousal RRSP makes more sense for us. I know I've never saved a dime in my life, but after experiencing first-hand what it's like to be without money, I never want to feel helpless and dependent again, either at retirement or two years from now.

"Until a minute ago, I believed that paying off the mortgage was the best form of security. Now I personally know why the RRSP is better. I like the fact that the RRSP is financially ahead of paying down the mortgage, but for me, the income security — the emergency buffer as you put it — is more important. Lisa and I would be able to relax and feel more secure knowing that another layoff would not threaten us financially."

"And of course, if you never needed the RRSP for emergency income, your retirement would be that much nicer," Scott alertly added.

Pierre's distant expression indicated that he was still thinking about something from earlier in the conversation. "Let me see if I understand this," he said. "There are times when you are further ahead to pay down debts than contribute to an RRSP. I guess what I am trying to figure out is what is the best way to invest my first available dollar, whether I have an extra hundred, or inherit $100,000."

"The **most effective use of your first available dollar**," I explained, "is to **pay down expensive non-deductible debt** — credit cards, personal loans, mortgages, whatever — whenever the interest is, say, over thirteen percent. Doing that will produce a guaranteed before-tax return of over twenty percent. Once that is done, you would be best off to **maximize your RRSPs**, investing in several Canadian equity mutual funds."

"And if you still had money to invest after contributing the maximum to your RRSP?" Pierre asked softly.

The three of us turned and looked at Pierre as if he had just landed from another planet.

"Business is really struggling, eh, Pierre?" Scott surmised.

"Oh, it's my parents who need to know, not me," he quickly defended himself. His startled reply made it difficult to say if he was telling the truth.

"Then I would invest in **international and American equity funds** for higher returns that are mostly capital gains," I advised.

"Which means the returns are taxed less than regular interest," Rob added, proud of his new financial awareness.

"But if you were more interested in investment income, as opposed to growth, would you consider **dividend funds** for a higher after-tax return?" Pierre asked.

"That's one good option to look at," I replied. "I read somewhere that, with the dividend tax credit, you could make over $23,000 in dividends without paying any tax, if that was your only income."

"As it might be for someone who is retired," Pierre noted. Maybe it really was his parents he was talking about.

"Rob, if you're starting an RRSP with mutual funds, you should be aware of one thing I just learned that was kind of interesting," I said.

"What's that?"

"I was surprised to discover that most mutual funds don't report how well your investment has done," I elaborated. "The annual statement tells you how many units of the fund you own, when you bought them, and all of the transaction details, but it doesn't give you the most important number — the average annual return."

"I was disappointed to discover that as well," Pierre agreed. "I don't know about you, but to me, keeping score in the investment game is pretty important, and the annual return is the only real way to compare the performance of different types of investments."

"What are you guys talking about?" Scott demanded. "I've seen mutual fund tables in the newspapers. They tell you the returns for the funds over different time periods."

"The tables do report how well *the fund* has done," I acknowledged, "but not how well *your* investment in the fund has done. Unless you bought only once at exactly one, three, five, or ten years ago, you only have a rough idea of how well *you* have done. Even then the tables don't give you the returns after taking into account commissions. And they don't help you at all if you bought at different times, which is certainly the case with a monthly investment plan.

"It's also valuable to know your returns when you are thinking about selling, so you try to sell high. That's why I put together a simple computer program to help me keep track of our mutual funds and, more importantly, know how well they're doing. You just enter the transaction details, and it figures out your real annual returns and keeps track of everything."

"I'd like to see that program," Pierre said. "Knowing how well you're doing also keeps you motivated and lets you know you're on the right track."

"Maybe in a year or so we can punch my numbers into the program to see how well I've done," Rob said. "Right now, I just want to get things started."

★ ★ ★

Later that fall, Scott, Kim, and Rachel showed up at our house unannounced, early in the morning, even for a Saturday.

"Scott, what's up? You seem unusually happy. Did the Leafs win again last night?"

"No, I've got some good news."

"What's that?"

"I'm definitely buying a house," he declared. "The apartment isn't big enough anymore."

"That's great. So you decided to bite the bullet and join the world of endless mortgage payments and debt," I kidded, ". . . ah, . . . I mean start a highly-leveraged, forced savings plan into one of the better investments — real estate."

Scott continued to glow, unfazed by my kidding. "That's not the real news. The real news is why it's not big enough anymore."

"What do you mean? Quit beating around the bush. Did you buy another toy that's too big to fit in the apartment?"

"No, it's better than that. I inherited a family. Kim and I are getting married!"

"Congratulations!" Theresa and I shouted out in unison, not really surprised by the announcement.

"Welcome to the club," I told Scott. "You couldn't have picked a better wife."

"Of course, you two will be standing up with us," Kim interjected.

"For sure. When is the big day?" Theresa asked.

"Later in the spring," Kim replied. "We'll be picking a date in the next few days."

"Well, we're really happy for the three of you," I said, smiling at Rachel.

After discussing some of the plans for the wedding and calming down from all of the excitement, Scott continued, "Since we're going to be getting a house, I wanted to get together with you sometime soon to brush up on some of the things we talked about last year: what I should know before buying a house, and how to reduce the mortgage costs. Oh, and life insurance too. I'll be needing some now that I have dependents." He smiled affectionately down at Rachel, before turning back to me. "You sure have learned a lot about managing money."

"I don't know about a lot," I said. "I'm sure there's much more to learn, but things have changed a lot from a year and a half ago when my uncle died and I discovered I was financially illiterate. By learning a few basics, we've saved thousands of dollars on insurance, on the minivan, and just by being better consumers in general. And over time, we will save tens of thousands in mortgage interest."

"The thing I like best," Theresa jumped in, "is that nothing we have done has sacrificed our standard of living — no budgeting, no counting pennies, just more money to spend as we see fit."

"Before we started talking about these things," Scott began, "I always thought that financial planning meant investing, and since I never had any money to invest, I never thought about it. Now I know there's much more to it than saving for retirement."

"You're right," I agreed. "Financial planning means taking care of all financial matters so you have money for whenever you need it, whether it's for a vacation, an education, or to make ends meet when you're between jobs as Rob was. And by being a better consumer, not only do you stop wasting money unnecessarily, you also end up with more money to invest."

"Or to start investing," Kim added.

"Or start investing," I echoed. "Before we learned how to get the same things for less, we didn't have any investments, only debt, which often results in stress. Now, as long as we continue our pay-yourself-first RRSP plans, our financial future is secure.

"And thanks to Pierre helping me start a part-time business, I have more extra work than I have time for, so I'm not totally dependent on my job for security. It really makes you stop and think, when you realize that if you aren't taking advantage of every financial opportunity, you're unnecessarily giving away your hard-earned money — to someone you don't even know."

"It's also comforting to know that our kids will never be financially illiterate, as we were," Theresa added. "That will give them a big advantage in today's money-oriented world."

"Well, Kim and I are glad you've opened our eyes to the benefits of a little financial knowledge and planning," Scott admitted sincerely. "I'll bet that most people are just like us and could benefit from learning some of the basics and, as you say, applying a little common sense."

"It's really too bad they don't teach this stuff in school," Kim remarked.

"I'm sure someday they will," I said. "But for now, we'll have to take care of it ourselves."

"Well, we're running late," Scott said, tossing Rachel up into his arms.

"Yes," Kim smiled, "we have a lot of people to see who don't know about the news."

"I'll be over sometime this week and we'll talk," Scott called over his shoulder.

"All right, we'll see you then."

Shortly after lunch, Theresa answered the phone and handed it to me. It was Phil from Kool's restaurant downtown. He wanted me to meet him there, so I agreed to stop in after running a few errands.

"Hi, Phil. What's up?"

"Talbot, can I buy you a beer?" he offered.

"Of course," I nodded, puzzled by the rare offer.

"A few months ago, we talked about a few ways to save money. Then I started talking to some of my friends. Talbot, I'd like you to meet Jeff and Debbie Chen," he said, pointing to the couple beside me.

"Nice to meet you."

"They tell me that by improving their insurance in just a few of the areas you told me about," Phil announced, "they've started saving sixty dollars a month."

"Over $700 a year," Deb clarified.

"Great," I said. "I'm glad it helped."

"The reason I asked you to stop in," Phil continued, "was because these two really appreciated the advice and wanted to learn more."

"We want to use the extra money to start an investment plan. We were thinking about RRSPs," Jeff said. "Phil said that mutual funds are a good idea."

"And we're also saving for a house," Deb added. "Do you have a minute to answer a few questions?"

I checked the time, nodded, and in the tradition of my retired financial mentor, replied, "Sure, we can talk as long as you want — as long as you're buying!"

Part Two

Quick Reference Strategies
With Real-Life Examples

How to Use the
Quick Reference Strategies

The *Quick Reference Strategies* serve many purposes.

- They form a **checklist** of over 150 strategies, including many not mentioned in Part One. This summary of **action strategies** allows you to quickly identify the ideas that apply to you personally, so you can act on them and start benefiting. Remember that *knowing* how to save $300 doesn't benefit you — until you *act* on it.

- They include **real-life examples** that quantify the benefit of acting on the strategies. People like to quote the examples when they are telling their friends what they have learned. Real examples emphasize the importance of the ideas and make them easier to relate to. Note that the names used in the examples are fictional, for illustration purposes only.

- They are an **index** to the strategies that are explained in more detail in Part One.

- They serve as a **future reference** for when your circumstances change, or as a periodic refresher to make sure you continue to do what you can to reduce expenses and invest effectively.

More Strategies?

In this quickly changing information age, new consumer and investor strategies arise every day. If you have an idea not listed here that will benefit most Canadians by at least $100 *without* lowering their standard of living, we would like to share it with others. Please send your strategy, with a real-life example of the benefits, to:

Financial Success Strategies Inc.
42 Fawn Court
London, Ontario N5X 3X3

Graphical Symbols

A number of the strategies have a graphical symbol beside them to help you identify their most important characteristic. Visually, these symbols allow you to quickly identify the different types of strategies as explained below.

BIG benefit

Continuing benefit

Easy

Cut costs

Cash back

Cut taxes

Increase security

Higher investment returns

Note

Free Up Money Without Sacrifice

PRACTICAL CONSUMER STRATEGIES

❏ **Shop around** for everything. Get at least **three quotes** for every major purchase. Prices for the same product can vary by as much as 200%. *p. 43*

- Remember that **$1 saved is $2 earned**. You must earn almost $2 to take home $1 after paying taxes, CPP, UI, benefits and other deductions. *p. 40*
- Because shopping around takes only minutes with the Yellow Pages, you can **earn hundreds of dollars an hour**. *p. 43*
- Use brokers, especially for insurance, investments, and mortgages. *p. 66*

> Examples:
> - James found a 0.5% lower rate on his $100,000 mortgage, saving about $35 a month or over $2,000 on a 5-year term.
> - Just by shopping around, Beth lowered her car insurance from $1,100 to $700. She gained $400 in fifteen minutes, or $1,600 an hour.
> - Instead of Canada Savings Bonds, Carmen bought cashable GICs paying 0.5% higher.

❏ **Buy slightly used** instead of new (homes, automobiles, furniture, appliances, etc.). This can also save the GST. *p. 80*

> Example: Sheri bought a quality, used dining room suite for $600 instead of $1,200, saving $600.

❏ **Negotiate**. Don't automatically pay the 'suggested' list price. Ask for a discount or something free. Talk to the manager and offer 10% less. *p. 86*

> Examples:
> - By shopping around and negotiating, Antonio bought a $2,200 stereo for $1,500, saving $700.
> - Carmen asks the store to pay the GST.

❏ Know how much **smoking** damages your financial health. The total cost of smoking 1 pack a day over different time periods is shown below. *p. 83*

Cost of Smoking 1 Pack of Cigarettes per Day					
Years	10	20	30	40	50
Cost	$25,000	$135,000	$500,000	$1,800,000	$5,800,000

Note: This table assumes that cigarettes cost $3.00 a pack, the cost will increase 10% a year, and the savings are invested at 10%. If cigarettes cost $6.00 a pack, double these figures. According to the Non-Smokers' Rights Association, the average increase in the cost of cigarettes in the 1980s was 14.7% per year.

> Example: Mike, a 35-year-old, quits smoking and invests the cost of one pack a day at 10% returns. Without doing anything else, he will have $500,000 30 years later.

❏ Understand **commission-based sales**. *p. 32*

- Don't be too trusting. Never assume that commissioned salespeople are acting in your best interest. They are paid different commissions for different products.

❏ Don't buy **extended warranties** (on vehicles, appliances, furniture, etc.). They are overpriced insurance policies. Cancel existing warranties for an immediate refund. *p. 81*

❏ Do not spend more than entertainment value on **lottery tickets** and **bingos**. Only about 60% of the money taken in by lotteries is paid out in prizes. Thus, over the long run, you can expect a return of negative 40%.

> Example: According to Statistics Canada, in 1990, the average household spent over $150 on lottery tickets. If you invested this amount every year at 10% interest, 25 years later you would have almost $15,000. How many lottery players have won this much?

❑ **Take a lunch** instead of buying (lower quality) food at a restaurant or cafeteria.

> Examples:
> • Sara brings pop from home instead of paying $1 at work and saves about $130 a year.
> • Paul takes his entire lunch and saves $400 a year.

❑ **Buyer Beware!** Realize that companies exist to make a profit.

• If it sounds too good to be true, it probably is.

• If you don't understand it, maybe you shouldn't buy it (yet).

• A verbal contract isn't worth the paper it's written on.

❑ In a two-income family, try to get one spouse's **benefits in extra salary** instead of wasting them through duplication.

❑ Buy in bulk and get a **volume discount**. Instead of buying canned and dry goods one at a time, buy by the case to save time and money.

❑ **Buy *more* on sale**. When non-perishable goods go on sale (often below cost), buy several months worth.

> Example: If a case of pop is regularly $9.99, and it is on special for $5.99, buy 5 cases (or enough to last until the next sale) and save $20.

❑ **Barter**. Trade favours with friends and neighbours to avoid paying income tax, GST, and PST. Note that goods or services related to your occupation are subject to tax.

> Example: In return for some baby-sitting, Betty's neighbour watched the house and garden while she was on vacation. No money changed hands or was lost to taxes.

❑ Buy at **auctions** for 30% – 90% off retail. *p. 80*

❑ Shop at **discount stores** or factory outlets.

❏ **Buy out of season** to get discounts of 50% or more.

❏ Use the right type of **bank services**:
- One **interest-paying chequing account** is easier to manage and may be the most profitable. *p. 78*
- Check the real value of your bank **service plan**. *p. 79*
- Use only one or two low- or **no-fee credit cards**.

❏ Consider **last-minute flight sell offs** for vacations and save hundreds of dollars. *p. 7*

❏ Get a 40% rebate on air fares if you fly to the funeral of a relative by supplying a copy of the death certificate.

❏ Most contracts signed as a result of a salesperson coming unsolicited to your door can be nullified during the first 48 hour **'cooling off' period**. *p. 86*

❏ Consider **long distance plans** if you have large long distance bills.

❏ Maintain a **list of useful gifts** for Christmas, etc. *p. 82*

BUYING A CAR

❏ Buy a one- or **two-year-old car** and save thousands of dollars. Cars depreciate about 30% in the first year and 25% in the second, yet the difference in appearance between a new car and one that is a year old is almost undetectable. You will also pay less GST and PST, as well as lowering insurance costs. *p. 55*
- **Private sales** generally offer the best bargain.
- Buying **privately** also **saves the 7% GST**, which is charged when you buy a used (or new) car from a dealer.
- Consider a **demonstration vehicle** from a dealer, or buying through an auto worker's employee car purchase plan for 10% - 20% off.

Example: By buying a one-year-old car in mint condition, instead of a new one, Marcel saved $6,000. This also meant borrowing $6,000 less, which saved an additional $1,500 in interest, for a total savings of $7,500.

❏ Consider taking a **taxi** or bus instead of buying a rarely used second vehicle.

Buying a New Car

❏ Sell your used vehicle yourself. At least don't announce that you have a **trade-in** until you finalize the new car's price. *p. 53*

❏ **Negotiate.** Dealers have lots of profit margin to work with (5% – 15%). Call a 'no-haggle' dealer for a reference price. *p. 53*

❏ Don't buy the **extended warranty.** *p. 54*

❏ Don't buy the **rustproofing** warranty. *p. 53*

❏ Don't buy the **life and disability loan insurance.** *p. 55*

❏ Shop around hard. Shop separately for financing. *p. 54*
  - Dealers outside of major cities are generally more competitive.
  - Buy in September when new models come out, or in December when dealers want to clear out last year's models.
  - Buy at the end of the month when salespeople may want your sale to improve their monthly performance or achieve a bonus.

❏ Don't buy **fabric protection** from the dealer. Do it yourself. *p. 54*

❏ Don't buy **paint sealant.** Wax it yourself. *p. 54*

Example: By not taking the $250 paint protection package and the $150 fabric protection, Natasha saved $400.

SAVE THOUSANDS ON INSURANCE COSTS

❑ **Only insure against major losses** that you cannot afford to pay for yourself. On average, any type of insurance is more expensive than paying for your own accidents because your premiums must also cover the cost of sales commissions, administrative fees, and overhead.

❑ **Shop around**. Rates can vary as much as 200% for the same coverage. *p. 43*

> Example: Jeff was paying $3,000 for car insurance. After a phone call, he is now paying only $2,000 for the same coverage and saves $1,000 every year.

❑ Don't buy **low-value insurance**. Cancel these coverages and get a refund:

- Credit card or personal loan life and disability insurance.
- Most **extended warranties** on cars, appliances, furniture, etc. *p. 81*

> Examples:
> - Roger borrowed $11,000 to buy a car and paid an additional $405 for life and disability insurance to cover the loan. Cancelling this insurance produced a refund of over $300.
> - By not buying the fabric protection and extended warranty on a couch and love-seat, Tim saved $150. Two cans of furniture protectant cost him $15.

❑ Increase the elimination period (when you start receiving benefits) on **disability insurance**. Most people have group disability coverage through work and/or worker's compensation. You may also get benefits from unemployment insurance (up to 15 weeks), CPP (for severe long-term disability), and auto insurance.

- A spouse who works, or who can work, is also a form of disability insurance.
- Read the fine print when shopping around.

Example: Bill, 35, paid $1,065 a year for a $2,000-a-month policy with a 30-day elimination period. By increasing the elimination period to 120 days, the premiums dropped 44%, saving $470 a year.

❏ If you pay for any insurance monthly, find out the **effective interest rate** charged. *p. 96*

Example: Some companies multiply the yearly premium by 0.09 to get the monthly premium. This equates to an interest charge of 18.6%.

Life Insurance

One of the most common areas of major financial mistakes is life insurance. The result is overpaying your premiums by thousands of dollars, inadequate protection or both. Many Canadians can reduce their life insurance expense by hundreds of dollars every year *and* increase their protection.

❏ **Do not buy** life insurance **unless you need it**. You need life insurance to provide income for dependents if you die. *p. 21*

❏ Do **not** buy life insurance **for children**, or as an education savings plan. *p. 24*

Example: Sofia cancelled the life insurance policy on her 2-year-old child and saved $110 a year.

❏ **Save** up to 50% on life insurance **if you do not smoke**. *p. 24*

• Check old policies to see if you are getting a significant discount for not smoking.

• If you quit smoking, get non-smoker rates.

Example: Henri, 45, paid $535 a year for $100,000 of term insurance. When he told his agent he had quit smoking, his premiums dropped to $270, saving $265 a year, or almost 50%.

Don't Buy Whole Life Insurance

❑ Don't buy whole life insurance, which is basically a combination of pure life insurance and a savings plan. *p. 17*

- Whole life is the **most expensive** coverage you can get. The same amount of whole life coverage can cost over 5 times as much as term insurance! A worse consequence is that because it is so expensive, you may not be able to afford adequate protection.

  Example: An agent tried to sell a doctor a $500,000 whole life policy costing $3,300 a year. She is now getting the same coverage with term insurance for $370 a year through her medical association, saving about 90% or $2,900 a year.

- Whole life is the best product for the agent and the company, not the consumer. They make the most money selling whole life insurance. *p. 32*

  Example: A 35-year-old father needs $250,000 of coverage. If the agent sells term insurance, the premiums would be about $360 a year and the agent would get a commission of about 50% of that or $180. If she sells whole life, the premiums would be about $1,200, and she would get a commission of about 100% of the first year's premium. Thus, the agent can make over 6 times as much by selling whole life instead of term insurance.

- You pay for both the insurance and the savings, but you **can only** possibly **get one**. If you die, you get the face value of the policy and the company keeps your cash values. To get your cash value, you must be alive and cancel the policy. *p. 18*

- Whole life insurance is very difficult to understand and compare.

❑ **Don't use** life insurance **as an investment**. The rate of return on the investment portion of whole life policies is very poor and is negative for the first few years. Also, you cannot get the investment portion without either:

- Borrowing from your policy and paying interest on your own money and, at the same time, reducing your coverage by an equal amount, OR
- Cashing in the policy, which means you no longer have coverage. *p. 33*

❑ Most people should not buy **universal life** policies, which are like flexible whole life policies where you get both the protection and the savings. You will generally get better insurance and investments by buying separately. *p. 33*

- Expensive commissions reduce investment growth.
- Withdrawal penalties limit your flexibility and control.

❑ Most people should **replace** their expensive **whole and universal life policies** with term insurance. *p. 26*

- Invest any cash values and savings achieved through lower premiums.
- **NOTE:** Do not cancel a policy until you have the replacement in place.

> Example: George was paying $1,100 a year for $100,000 of whole life insurance. By switching to term insurance, he saved $700 a year *and* tripled his coverage.

Buy Only Term Life Insurance

❑ Most people should buy only term life insurance and invest the savings. *p. 17*

- It is the **lowest-cost** protection you can get, especially when you need the most insurance (starting a family).
- Term life insurance is **simple**. Understanding it puts you in control.

❑ Only buy **automatically renewable** and convertible term insurance. *p. 26*

❑ Buy a policy value that is **5 to 10 times** your current **income**, plus outstanding debts. This will provide 50% – 100% of your income when invested at 10%. Review your needs every 5 years, or when your circumstances change. *p. 22*

> Example: Angela is a single parent earning $30,000 and has a $100,000 mortgage. She should have at least $250,000 of life insurance (5 x $30,000 + $100,000).

❑ Buy only pure term life insurance, without expensive bells and whistles.

- Get only **non-participating** term insurance. *p. 27*
- Don't buy **accidental death** or double indemnity riders. Your insurance needs do not increase if you die accidentally.
- Don't buy **waiver of premium** riders. *p. 27*

❑ **Don't buy** term insurance with **long terms** (term-to-65, term-to-100, etc.). You are paying more than you need to for something you may not need later. Five- or ten-year terms are generally the best buy. *p. 26*

> Example: Instead of buying $100,000 of term-to-100 insurance for $790 a year, 45-year-old Carlos bought a 5-year term policy for $305 a year, and saved 60% or $485 a year.

❑ Most people can **reduce** their **coverage** as they get older with fewer dependents, less debt, and more assets. *p. 26*

- If you want to pass certain investments (like real estate, stocks, equity mutual funds, or a business) to your survivors, consider a term-to-100 or a good universal life insurance policy to pay for the capital gains taxes that are due at death. *p. 34*

❑ Calculate the **unit cost** to determine the best value. Divide the annual premium by the coverage to get the annual cost per thousand dollars of insurance.

Example: $50,000 of insurance for $150 a year has a unit cost of 150/50 = $3 per thousand. $300,000 of insurance for $300 a year has a unit cost of 300/300 = $1 per thousand, and is a much better value.

❏ Buy **mortgage life insurance** only if it is a better value than term insurance. Mortgage life insurance only pays off the balance of the mortgage which decreases in value each year. *p. 27*

- Replace declining-value mortgage life insurance with term insurance when term insurance is a better value.

❏ Compare **group term** life insurance rates available from alumni or professional associations, or through work. Note that group insurance might not cover you when you leave the company or association.

Car Insurance

❏ **Raise** the **collision deductible** on your automobile policy to $500 or more.

- Most people won't make small claims anyway for fear that premiums will go up.
- A higher deductible gives you incentive to drive carefully, since an accident that is your fault will cost you more. *p. 44*

Example: Kathryn saved $110 a year by increasing her collision deductible from $250 to $1,000.

❏ **Raise** the **comprehensive deductible** on your automobile policy to $100 or more. *p. 44*

Example: Raising his comprehensive deductible from $50 to $250 saves Jack $34 a year.

❏ Never file a **small collision claim** (less than $500). After paying the deductible, you gain very little, while damaging your driving record and potentially increasing your rates either immediately or in the future. *p. 44*

❏ **Shop** around **every year** or two. *p. 43*

- Find out how much an accident or ticket will raise your premiums, before they happen.

> Example: By shopping around at renewal, Pam saved another $100 a year.

❏ **Drop** collision and comprehensive **coverage** when the value of the automobile drops below $2,000. *p. 45*

❏ Get these **discounts** if you meet low-risk criteria: abstainer, live close to work, senior citizen, good driving record, driver education, own several vehicles. *p. 45*

- You may (and should) get a discount for: being a non-smoker, anti-theft devices, air bags, anti-lock brakes, permanence of residence.

❏ In Ontario, **pay** car insurance premiums **monthly** instead of annually. The maximum interest charge allowed by law in Ontario is 3%. *p. 46*

Home and Tenant Insurance

❏ **Increase the deductible** to $500 or more instead of the usual $200, and reduce premiums by 15% – 25%. *p. 46*

> Example: Dan's home insurance went down 15% or $35 a year after increasing the deductible from $200 to $500.

❏ When shopping around, ask for **discounts** if you've never made a claim, have a newer home or burglar alarm, don't smoke, or carry car insurance with same company. *p. 46*

❏ **Don't insure for more than you own.** Only insure the cost of replacing the buildings and contents. *p. 46*

> Example: Tony had $40,000 coverage for his apartment even though he only owned about $10,000 of possessions. This was costing him an extra $50 a year for something he could never get.

CUT MORTGAGE COSTS BY 30% – 50%

For most people, a home is the largest investment they make. To put the cost in perspective, consider the fact that a standard 25-year $100,000 mortgage at 12% interest will cost more than $309,000.

Because saving $1 is the same as earning $2, someone in the top tax bracket will have to earn over $600,000 to pay off that $100,000 debt. However, using a few of the strategies below, you can cut the total interest cost *in half* — *without* lowering your standard of living!

Note that all examples in this section assume a mortgage amount of $100,000. To relate the examples to your own situation, multiply or divide the savings as appropriate. For example, if you have a $200,000 mortgage, double the savings shown in the strategies below.

Purchases and Renewals

❏ Pay **bi-weekly or weekly** instead of monthly to save tens of thousands of dollars in interest. By paying half of the normal monthly payment every two weeks, you automatically pay off the mortgage a little faster. *p. 67*

> Example: A $100,000, 12%, 25-year mortgage that is paid weekly or bi-weekly is paid off in 17.5 years. This cuts the total interest cost by 36%, **saving over $76,000.**

❏ **Amortize** for **15 or 20 years**, not the normal 25. Your payments will be negligibly higher, but your interest savings will be substantial. *p. 68*

> Example: At 10% interest, amortizing for 20 years instead of 25 increases your payments by only 6%, yet reduces the total interest cost by 24%. On a $100,000 mortgage, the difference in monthly payments is only $57, but you **save $40,000 in total interest**.

❏ **Increase** your **payments** each year as your income increases to cut your total interest cost in half! This approach gives you the best of both worlds, because your payments are as low as possible at the start and you save the maximum interest *without* sacrifice. By increasing the payments at the same rate that your income increases, you do not lower your standard of living at all. *p. 68*

> Examples:
> - A 12%, $100,000, 25-year mortgage is paid off in 12 years and 3 months by simply increasing the monthly payment 5% every year. This cuts the total interest paid by 51%, **saving over $105,000!**
> - Paying the above mortgage weekly and increasing the payments only 2% each year is an easier way to save over $100,000 in interest.

❏ For those who want to **do it all**, pay bi-weekly or weekly, reduce the amortization period, and increase your payments every year.

> Example: Raoul borrows $100,000 at 10% interest, but hates having a mortgage hanging over his head. By reducing the amortization period slightly to 20 years, paying weekly, and increasing his payments each year by only 3%, he **saves over $92,000**. The total interest paid is 55% less than with the normal 25-year monthly mortgage.

❏ Make **lump-sum prepayments** against the principal, especially early in the mortgage.

> Example: A single $1,000 contribution at the end of the first year of a 25-year $100,000 mortgage at 12% saves over $14,000 in interest.

❏ Finance for **shorter terms** (one year, two years, or open) unless you have little equity in the house and cannot afford the possibility of higher interest rates. You generally pay a hefty premium for the security of longer terms. Five-year rates can be 1% − 2% higher than one-year rates. In the 1980s, the average rate for one-year closed mortgages was 12.6%, and the average rate for five-year mortgages was 13.6%. *Source: Bank of Canada. p. 71*

> Example: On a $100,000 mortgage, averaging 1% lower interest by choosing one-year terms instead of five-year terms saves over $800 a year, or $20,000 in total interest.

- Consider a **variable rate mortgage** if rates are high and expected to drop, and you can afford to end up owing more if rates go up. Interest rates on variable mortgages can be 2% lower than five-year rates.

❑ **Shop around** initially and at each renewal.
- Consider a mortgage **broker** to help you shop around and explain your options. *p. 62*
- Be careful of hidden costs. Read the fine print.

❑ Consider the **Granny mortgage** if you have the opportunity. Granny, or anyone you trust, can 'gift' $100,000 to you, and you can 'gift' $1,000 a month to her without any tax consequences. As long as they are gifts and not a loan with interest payable, Granny does not have to pay tax on this income. Many people simply calculate a regular mortgage payment at a lower rate. **Note**: Legally, tax must be paid on the interest portion of the payment.

> Example: You have a $100,000 mortgage at 12% and your aunt is earning 10% with a GIC (6% after tax). If she lends you the money at 9%, then both of you benefit by 3%, or $3,000 a year.

❑ Use a **Granny loan** to get a 25% down payment to **save** the Canadian Mortgage and Housing Corporation **(CMHC) payment insurance**, which can cost as much as 2.5%, and is not refundable. *p. 73*

❑ If you do not have a 25% down payment, get a **second mortgage** instead of paying CMHC insurance for the first mortgage, *if* you can pay off the second mortgage in less than 5 years. *p. 73*

❏ If rates are dropping, **don't miss** out on **mortgage rate drops** that occur even on the day of closing.

❏ **Don't** pay a penalty to **refinance** before the end of the term unless you are sure you will benefit. Get your lender or a professional with mortgage software to evaluate the options accurately. *p. 66*

- Generally, paying an interest rate differential penalty is not profitable, while paying a penalty of three months' interest can be a smart move if rates have fallen enough.

- Any CMHC-insured mortgage can be repaid after the third year of a fixed term by paying a penalty of three months' interest.

❏ Refuse to pay **mortgage renewal fees**. Tell your lender that the competition would gladly pay the renewal fee to get the business. *p. 65*

❏ Don't let the lender pay your **property taxes**. They often hold more money than they need to and pay you little or no interest.

Upgrading Your Home

❏ Get a **guaranteed rebate** and save hundreds every time you buy or sell real estate by calling the **Canadian Transfer Association** at **1-800-465-1198**. Simply call CTA when you are going to move and let them call the real estate office to get you an agent (possibly one you suggest). CTA's referring realtor receives a referral fee, which it shares with you. You get a refund of 0.3%, or $3 per $1,000 of the total transaction. *p. 87*

> Example: If you sold a $100,000 home and bought a $200,000 home, the CTA would send you a cheque for $300,000 x 0.3% = $900.

❏ **Try selling** your home **yourself** and save the (6%) sales commission, especially if you are not in a hurry to sell. There are books to help you sell a home yourself. *p. 88*

Example: Using word of mouth, putting a few flyers up at work, and holding two open houses, Harold sold his $120,000 home without an agent and saved $7,200.

❏ **Sell before buying** to avoid the panic sell.

RRSP or Pay Down Mortgage?

❏ Most people are financially further ahead to **contribute to an RRSP** unless their mortgage rate is at least 3% higher than their average RRSP return. For example, if RRSPs average 10%, only pay down debts charging 13% or more. This assumes that you will invest two-thirds of your mortgage payments in your RRSP after the mortgage is paid off. *p. 164*

• If you will invest less than two-thirds of the payments when the mortgage is gone, then the RRSP should come ahead of even more expensive debts.

Example: Both Mark and Rose have 15 years left on $100,000 mortgages charging 12%. Both have $4,000 a year to invest, and average 10% RRSP returns. Mark hates debt and uses his $4,000 a year to pay off the mortgage and then start his RRSPs. Rose invests her $4,000 a year in an RRSP. If they invest only half of their mortgage payment when the mortgage is paid off, 30 years later Rose's RRSP will be worth $155,000 more than Mark's.

• If you will invest all of the mortgage payments after, then if your RRSP averages 10%, you are mathematically ahead paying down any debt charging 8% or more.

Example: If they invested *all* of their payments after paying off the mortgage, Mark, who paid down the mortgage first, would have a retirement fund $210,000 larger than Rose's.

❏ Most people should contribute to an RRSP, regardless of the mortgage rate, for other reasons.

- RRSPs provide more real **security** and **peace of mind**. They can be used as an **emergency fund** or income insurance for low- or no-income periods, when they can be withdrawn to cover expenses with little or no tax payable. *p. 165*

- RRSPs are **more liquid**, increase your total **diversification**, and lead to more investment options (See strategies on withdrawing RRSPs tax-free). *p. 165*

- RRSPs produce a **tax refund** for extra short-term cash flow.

- RRSPs are **additional forced savings**, especially when you invest monthly. *p. 164*

DEBT REDUCTION STRATEGIES

❑ **Refinance fixed-rate personal loans** when rates drop. There are generally no penalties for refinancing or prepaying personal loans. *p. 76*

> Example: Jamie borrowed $10,000 at 15% interest to buy a car. A year later, rates dropped 3%. Refinancing at 12% for the last 3 years of the 4-year term saved him $420.

❑ **Refinance expensive** credit card **debt** with a lower rate personal loan. *p. 107*

> Example: Refinancing a $5,000 17% credit card debt at 11% saves $300 per year.

❑ **Pay off your credit cards** in full, and use the bank's money for over a month interest free. *p. 97*

❑ Consider a **low-rate credit card** if you don't pay your balance off every month. Watch the annual fees.

❑ **Finance** personal debts over **2 or 3 years**, not the usual 4. *p. 54*

> Example: Michelle borrows $10,000 at 12% to buy a car. By financing for 3 years instead of 4, she saves $680 in interest.

HOMEOWNER COST REDUCTION STRATEGIES

❏ Install an energy-saving **setback thermostat** to save up to 15% on your heating costs.

❏ **Caulk, weatherstrip, and seal** windows and doors.

❏ **Upgrade insulation.**

❏ Install an **energy-saving shower head** and reduce the amount of water you use for showers by 30% – 50%.

❏ Consider replacing **electric water heaters** and electric clothes **dryers** with more economical natural gas appliances.

❏ Don't forget about the **interest on the security deposit** (last month's rent) and key deposits. Ontario law requires landlords to pay 6% interest on the last month's security deposit.

> Example: After 3 years, the interest on a $600 security deposit is $115.

❏ Reduce water bills by adding water-filled jars to your toilet's water reservoir, or by simply adjusting the float.

TAX REDUCTION STRATEGIES

General Tax Planning

❏ **Get professional help** to minimize your tax costs all year. Tax laws are too complicated and change too often. It does not make sense to save $50 by filing your own return if it ends up costing you $500 in errors, missed deductions and credits, and a lack of year-round tax reduction strategies.

  • Or keep up to date with a professional every other year, and do it yourself in between.

❏ **Investment counselling** and portfolio management is tax deductible. So are safety deposit box costs. *p. 155*

> Example: Janet hired an investment counsellor to get unbiased advice on how to improve her investments so that she could retire early. Because the $200 fee is tax deductible, she gets a refund of over $80.

❏ **Understand your tax return.** Work through your own at least once. *p. 154*

❏ Most people should **avoid tax shelters**, which offer tax deductions for making riskier investments. Their complexity breaks the 'Keep It Simple' rule, and spending $1 to save $0.50 in taxes doesn't make sense if you lose the dollar.

  • Only consider tax shelters if you are debt free, have maximized your RRSPs, and have seen a trusted professional.

Maximizing Deductions and Credits

❏ Don't miss **tax deductions or credits**.

  • Use the **general** income **tax form**, not the short or specials.

- Don't miss valuable **deductions**: moving expenses (including real estate agent commissions, legal and land transfer fees); medical costs if they exceed 3% of net income in any 12-month period; equivalent-to-married deduction; charitable donations; child care expenses; alimony and maintenance; educational expenses, etc. *p. 154*

❏ Have **old returns reassessed** if you discover a missed deduction, tax credit or change in your favour. Under the government's new Fairness Program, you can have any tax return within the past seven years reassessed. *p. 155*

> Example: Jim was promoted and moved to Toronto two years ago, but forgot to deduct $12,000 in moving expenses. Filing for a reassessment resulted in a refund cheque for $4,900.

Income Splitting

❏ Invest in the name of the **lower income earner**, so returns are taxed at the lowest possible rate. *p. 156*

❏ Contribute to a **spousal RRSP** if your spouse's income will be lower when the plan is cashed in (normally at retirement). *p. 117*

❏ You can **gift** money to anyone **over 18** (except your spouse) without income tax consequences on future investment income. Note: The recipient then owns the money.

❏ You can **gift** money to anyone **under 18**, and invest it for capital gains (via equity mutual funds or stocks) without the gains being taxed back to you. Any interest or dividend income is taxable in your name. *p. 152*

Starting Your Own Business

❑ Start a legitimate small business out of your home for additional **income**, increased **security**, and dozens of extra **tax deductions**. *p. 157*

- Start part-time to keep the security of your current job. *p. 157*
- If you don't have a marketable idea of your own, consider joining one of the many **network marketing** companies. *p. 158*

❑ Deduct everything related to the business, including:

- A portion of business-related **meals and entertainment**. *p. 158*
- The business portion of personal assets (computer, office furniture, etc.).
- A portion of total **home expenses** for a home office, including rent or mortgage interest, taxes, utilities, heat, and cleaning. *p. 158*

> Example: Jacques, a computer programmer, started consulting part-time. He makes additional income working when he wants, and his new tax deductions produced a refund of over $1,500.

❑ **Split income** with your spouse and children by paying them for legitimate business related activities. *p. 160*

> Example: Jacques pays his 10-year-old daughter $20 a week for stuffing envelopes, running errands, and cleaning the office. This is a tax deduction for him and eliminates the need to pay her an allowance.

❑ Register for the GST to avoid paying GST on business expenses.

❑ Call the Ministry of Economic Development & Trade or the Business Startup Hotline (1-800-567-2345 in Ontario) for more information.

- Ask what **government grants** and incentives are available. *p. 157*

HOW TO FREE UP EXTRA CASH TODAY

❑ Cancel your life insurance if you have no dependents. *p. 21*

❑ Cancel life insurance on children. *p. 24*

❑ Replace expensive whole or universal life insurance with low-cost term insurance. *p. 26*

❑ If you quit smoking, get lower non-smoker life insurance rates. *p. 24*

❑ Cancel life and disability insurance on personal loans, car loans, and credit cards, or replace with better-value coverage. *p. 55*

❑ Cancel low-value extended warranties (vehicle maintenance, vehicle rustproofing, appliance or furniture warranty). *p. 81*

❑ Shop around for all insurance protection and switch to better-value policies. *p. 43*

❑ Raise deductibles on car and home insurance policies. *p. 44*

❑ Increase the elimination period on disability insurance.

❑ Refinance fixed-rate personal loans when rates drop. *p. 76*

❑ Refinance expensive credit card debt with a personal loan at a lower rate. *p. 107*

❑ Reassess old tax returns and request a refund for missed deductions, credits, or omissions. *p. 155*

❑ Consider a low-rate credit card if you don't pay your balance off every month.

Successful Investment Strategies

THE MAGIC OF COMPOUND INTEREST

❑ Understand the power of **compound interest**. The *time value of money* is one of the most important and fundamental concepts. *p. 104*

> Example: If Ellen invests the cost of one pack of cigarettes ($3.00) a day at 10% interest, and the cost of cigarettes goes up 10% each year, she will have $1,800,000 after 40 years!

❑ Use the Universal Wealth Formula.

> **Savings x Time x Return = Wealth**

- You don't have to be born rich to become rich. Even small savings accumulate to significant sums over time.

> Example: Just $50 a month invested at 10% over 40 years grows to $280,000.

- It is easy to retire a millionaire!

> Example: To have $1 million at age 65, averaging only 8% returns, a 45-year-old needs to invest $1,760 a month; a 35-year-old needs to invest $710 a month; and a 25-year-old needs to invest only $310 a month.

❑ **Don't wait** to start investing. Procrastination is the investor's biggest enemy. Time is the most important of the three Wealth Formula factors. *p. 108*

> Example: At age 25, Terry the tortoise starts investing $2,000 a year for 40 years. At age 45, Harry the hare starts investing $4,000 for the next 20 years. Both invest the same $80,000, and average 8% interest. At age 65, Terry has $520,000 while Harry, the procrastinator, has only $180,000. Without investing a penny more, Terry has almost 3 times as much — an extra $340,000. Can you afford to wait?

❏ Use the **72 rule** to determine how fast money grows. Divide 72 by the interest rate to find the number of years it takes to double your money. *p. 107*

> Example: At 12% interest, your money doubles every 72/12 = 6 years. At 8%, it takes 9 years.

PAY YOURSELF FIRST TEN PERCENT

❏ **Set up a monthly investment program of at least 10% of your net income.** Pay the most important person first: *you*. This is the simplest, easiest, most painless way to save, because by automatically investing a small, regular amount, you never even miss the money. *p. 102*

  • Set up a Pre-Authorized Chequing (**PAC**) plan, or have your employer set up a **payroll deduction** so it comes off your paycheque before you get a chance to spend it.

> Example: John earns $40,000 and invests 10% of his income ($4,000 a year) at 10% interest. After 40 years, he has over $1,750,000.

❏ **Increase the amount of your regular investment as your income increases.** If you can invest 10% of your income now, and your income increases, you can increase your investment plan each year *without* lowering your standard of living. *p. 144*

> Example: Jane starts investing the same $4,000 a year as John, but increases the amount 4% each year as her income rises. After 40 years, she has $2,700,000 — almost a million dollars more — *without* sacrifice.

MAXIMIZE AFTER-TAX RETURNS

❏ Know the **marginal tax rate** for income and each type of investment, and invest in **tax-efficient investments**. Approximate tax brackets and rates follow. *p. 93*

Approximate Marginal Tax Rates				
Annual Income	0 – $6,500	$6,500 – $30,000	$30,000 – $60,000	over $60,000
Tax Rate	0%	27%	42%	53%

Example: Muriel is in the middle tax bracket. If she earns an extra $100, she will lose $42 to income taxes.

❑ Think in terms of **after-tax returns**, not before-tax returns. All that matters is how much you keep, not how much you share with the government. This is one of the most common investment errors. *p. 129*

• Always compare the after-tax returns of investment alternatives.

Example: For someone in the middle tax bracket, the after-tax return of a 10% GIC is less than 6%, since over 40% of the interest is lost to taxes.

❑ **Minimize interest income**. You can no longer earn $1,000 interest tax free, and it is taxed at your full marginal rate. *p. 129*

❑ For long-term investments, invest for **capital gains**, which are only taxed at 75% of your marginal tax rate. *p. 129*

• Use equity mutual funds, or stocks, where the returns are mostly capital gains.

• Capital losses can be applied against capital gains to reduce taxes.

• The $100,000 lifetime capital gains exemption was eliminated in 1994.

❑ Invest for **Canadian dividends**, especially if you need investment income, because with the Dividend Tax Credit, they are taxed at about two-thirds of your marginal tax rate. *p. 129*

• If dividends are your only income, you can earn over $23,000 a year tax-free. *p. 167*

• $1 of dividend income is the same as $1.25 of interest income.

> Example: A 10% GIC and an 8% dividend yield both produce the same after-tax return (about 6% for someone in the middle tax bracket).

❏ Understand how taxes affect all financial decisions. For someone in the middle tax bracket:
- If you earn an extra $100, $42 goes to taxes. *p. 114*
- $1,000 RRSP contribution produces a $420 tax refund. *p. 110*
- In Ontario, saving $1 on a purchase is really saving $1.15, because of the 8% PST and 7% GST. *p. 80*
- You need to earn $2 to keep $1, after paying taxes, CPP, UI, etc. Therefore, saving $100 is the same as earning an extra $200. *p. 40*

RRSPs – THE WEALTHBUILDER'S TAX SHELTER

An RRSP is a **multi-purpose tax shelter**, not a specific investment. Another misconception is that the entire RRSP fund belongs to you. The RRSP is **only partly yours**. Part belongs to the government in the form of deferred taxes. *p. 116*

❏ Contribute to an RRSP for a **tax refund** of up to 50% or more. *p. 110*

> Example: Since she is in the middle tax bracket, Susan's $1,000 RRSP contribution results in a tax refund of $420. Thus, the $1,000 investment really only cost $580.

❏ Use an RRSP for **tax-free compounding** to double or triple your retirement funds. The original investment and accumulated interest compounds tax-free until it is withdrawn, significantly enhancing growth. *p. 111*

> Example: $200 a month invested at 10% interest (6% after-tax) grows to $90,000 after 20 years. Assuming that the refunds were reinvested, the same investment inside an RRSP would grow to over $200,000.

❑ **Contribute the maximum** every year. *p. 115*
- Borrow if necessary, if you can repay the loan in a year or so.

❑ **Do not procrastinate** and rely on the carry-forward rules. *p. 115*
- **Invest every month** the easy, automatic way using a monthly Pre-Authorized Chequing (PAC) plan or payroll deductions. *p. 115*
- Contribute **early in the year**, not next February.

> Example: At 26, Ross invests $1,000 at 8%. At age 65, he will have $20,000. If he had started only one year earlier, he would have had 8% more, or an extra $1,600.

❑ Contribute to a **spousal RRSP** if your spouse's income will be lower when the plan is cashed in (normally at retirement). *p. 117*

> Example: Karen earns $150,000 with her medical practice. Her husband Ted earns $55,000 as a teacher. Since Ted has an excellent pension, and Karen has none, Ted should make the spousal contribution, to try to balance the two retirement incomes.

❑ **Shelter** your most **highly-taxed investments** inside your RRSP. If you have both interest-bearing and equity investments, hold the higher-taxed interest investments inside your RRSP. *p. 136*

❑ Build up an RRSP for **additional income security**. If your income stops because you are out of work or temporarily disabled, you can relax knowing that you can always make your mortgage payments by cashing some RRSPs as needed. *p. 165*

❑ Get your **tax refund immediately** by getting your employer to reduce your withholding tax, which increases your take-home pay now. Call Revenue Canada for the Waiver of Source Deductions form.

❑ Set up a **self-directed RRSP** when your total annual RRSP trustee fees exceed $100, or when you want to invest in something that requires it. *p. 121*

❑ When you're forced to (at age 69), **roll** your **RRSP into a RRIF** (Registered Retirement Income Fund). This allows it to continue compounding tax-free, while you maintain total control over how the funds are invested. *p. 117*

• Consider rolling some RRSP funds into an annuity if annuity interest rates are high. *p. 117*

Withdraw RRSPs Tax Free, or Taxed Less

❑ **Withdraw** RRSP funds **when your income is lower** — when retired, home raising a family, temporarily unemployed, starting a business, having a bad year in business, or taking time off for extended travel. *p. 119*

> Example: Jane plans to start a family. After building up a $15,000 RRSP, she stops working and starts withdrawing $4,000 a year. The withdrawals are totally tax-free because they are less than her basic personal exemption. Thus she avoids paying tax on the original contribution and accumulated interest, saving over $7,000 in taxes!

• Use RRSPs to take a **free vacation** anywhere in the world, paid for by the government. *p. 119*

> Example: Tom decides to take a year off to travel. If he builds up a $15,000 RRSP and cashes it in during the year off, he will only pay $2,300 in tax instead of 42% of $15,000, which is $6,300. The $4,000 tax savings is enough for a nice vacation anywhere in the world!

❑ Single income families should set up a **spousal RRSP**. Three years after the last spousal contribution, the spouse with no earnings can start cashing in about $6,500 of RRSPs each year tax-free, because of the basic personal exemption. *p. 120*

How to Earn 25% Interest or More *Guaranteed*

❏ **Pay off personal credit card debts** to earn a guaranteed return of 25% or more. This investment is **very profitable, guaranteed,** and **easy.** *p. 94*

- Over 25% return is excellent.

- You are guaranteed not to pay the high interest charges.

- The 'investment' is easy since the application form (credit card bill) is delivered right to your door.

> Example: A 25% GIC would leave you with 15% after paying taxes. Paying down a 15% credit card results in the same 15% after-tax return.

❏ Know the interest charged and pay down the **most expensive debt first**. Department store cards generally charge more than bank credit cards. *p. 96*

> Example: For someone in the middle income bracket, paying down a 29% department card debt is the same as investing in a 56% GIC.

- Understand how the **compounding frequency** affects the real interest rate charged. *p. 96*

> Example: Many department store cards charge 29% compounded *monthly*. This equates to an effective annual interest rate of 33% — a difference of 4% per year because of the one word 'monthly'.

❏ **Cash poorer investments** (those earning less than 25%), to pay down non-deductible credit card debt. *p. 96*

> Example: Joe's credit card balance averages $1,000, and he has GICs paying 8% interest. By cashing a $1,000 GIC and paying off the 17% card completely, Joe saves about $120 every year that his card balance stays at zero.

MUTUAL FUNDS FOR BETTER RETURNS

❏ Invest in **mutual funds** for **higher returns, professional management, diversification, liquidity** and more investment options. *p. 130*

- With many types available (equity, balanced, bond, money market, dividend, real estate, specialty), there is a fund for almost every investment objective. *p. 130*

- Equity mutual funds are the easy, safe, diversified way to take advantage of the higher long-term returns of the stock market. *p. 130*

- Mutual funds are for everyone, not just the wealthy. You can get started with as little as $50 a month. *p. 131*

❏ **How to Select a Mutual Fund**:

- Choose a fund **type** that matches your investment objectives. *p. 135*

- Find out who the **fund manager** is, and how long have they been there. *p. 146*

- Compare the funds' **past annual returns** (medium and long-term). *p. 146*

- Invest in **2 to 4** different mutual funds, for extra diversification. *p. 145*

- Find out about all **fees** (front, back, annual, administration, distribution, account setup, transfer, redemption) before you invest. *p. 146*

- Don't avoid a good **commission-based fund** for an average no-load fund. Your objective is to maximize your after-commission returns. There are some good no-load mutual funds, but you won't get any advice. The extra service from a financial planner alone may more than justify the commission. *p. 145*

Example: A 4% commission spread out over 10 years lowers your annual return by less than 0.5%. Some funds have returns 2% – 5% better than average.

HOW TO INCREASE INVESTMENT RETURNS

❑ Choose the **right type** of investment for the length of the investment to **minimize total risk.** *p. 135*

❑ For **long-term** investments (7 years or more), **own, don't loan.** Long-term ownership of stocks (equity funds) or real estate has outperformed interest paying investments for hundreds of years. 'Guaranteed' investments like **GICs provide short-term guarantees only,** and may guarantee that your long-term retirement fund is much less than it could be. *p. 128*

- **Fact:** For the 37-year period from 1950 to the end of 1987 (ending *after* the stock market crash), the average annual return for Canadian equities was 11.1%, while government-guaranteed bonds and treasury bills averaged between 5.2% and 6.2%. Thus the returns for 'guaranteed' investments averaged almost 5% less per year. *Source: James Hatch and Robert White, Canadian Stocks, Bonds, Bills and Inflation: 1950 - 1987.*

Example: Richard invests $4,000 a year in guaranteed investments that average 6% returns. Mary invests the same amount into equity mutual funds that average 10%. 30 years later, Richard has $315,000, but Mary has almost $660,000 — over twice as much. By insisting on investments with short-term guarantees, Richard risks having a retirement fund half as large as it could be.

- Don't move all of your retirement funds into guaranteed investments as soon as you retire. Some of the money won't be needed for 10 or 20 years, which is a long term. *p. 152*

❑ For **short-term** investments (less than 4 years), choose guaranteed, cash-type investments like **money market funds** or **GICs.** *p. 135*

❑ For medium-term investments, create a balance of cash, bonds, and some equities.

❑ Know the most effective place for your **first available dollar**. Follow this order. *p. 166*

1. Pay off **expensive non-deductible debt** (over 13%).

2. Maximize **RRSPs**. Use a spousal RRSP if your spouse will have a lower income when the money is withdrawn. Invest in Canadian equity or balanced mutual funds, if the investment is for at least 7 years.

3. Pay off **less expensive non-deductible debt** (less than 13%).

4. For long-term growth, invest for **capital gains** (international and American equity funds).

5. For investment income, invest for **Canadian dividends** which are taxed the least.

❑ **Diversify.** Don't put all your eggs in one basket, no matter what basket. *p. 145*

• Own more than one mutual fund.

• Create a balanced mix of cash, bonds, and equities, particularly as you get closer to retirement.

❑ **Invest regularly** to take advantage of **dollar cost averaging**. By investing the same amount at regular intervals, you automatically buy more shares when the price falls, and less when the price rises. This simple approach eliminates the need to try to time investments, and you automatically benefit in decreasing and fluctuating markets. *p. 132*

❑ Invest in **international** and **American** funds. Generally, American funds outperform Canadian funds, and international funds outperform American funds. *p. 141*

❑ Maximize your **foreign content limit** by investing up to 20% of your RRSP outside of Canada, for higher returns and extra diversification. *p. 141*

❑ Consider **small cap** funds, which invest in smaller, junior companies. The average growth of smaller companies is generally higher than that of large, blue-chip corporations.

❑ **Reinvest** all fund **dividends** for extra compound growth. *p. 141*

❑ **Buy (more) low** and **sell (some) high.** *p. 140*
- Be ready to buy more equity funds when they are 'on sale' during recessions, and often during the months of October and December.
- Consider selling (some) whenever the one- or two-year annual returns are more than double the long-term average. The next short-term returns will probably be below average to even out.

❑ **Don't buy high.** Don't make a lump-sum investment into the fund that just had the best one-year return. Although it will make very little difference over a 30-year period, the short-term returns may discourage you from sticking to your original long-term plan. *p. 140*

❑ If you want guaranteed investments, shop around for **cashable GICs**, which can be **1% higher** than Canada Savings Bonds. *p. 122*
- Buy small denominations so you can cash them slowly as needed.

Magnifying Returns Using Leverage

❑ Consider using leverage to magnify investment gains (and losses), the way the rich do. Generally, interest expenses incurred to invest are tax deductible. **Warning:** Leveraging should only be used by those comfortable with increased risk, financially able to handle the consequences, and knowledgeable in investing — *after* seeing a trusted financial advisor. *p. 142*

> Example: Doug, who is in the middle tax bracket, wants to invest $1,000 into equity mutual funds. He expects an annual return of 10%, and can borrow money for 10%. If he simply invests the money the normal way, he will earn $100 after one year (10%). If he uses the $1,000 as collateral to borrow another $1,000, he invests $2,000 which earns 10% or $200. For the year, borrowing the $1,000 cost $100 initially, but only $60 after the 40% tax deduction. Thus, the leveraged investment gains $200 - $60 = $140, for a return of 14%, 4% more than the unleveraged investment.

- **Real estate allows high leverage** because you can invest with as little as 5%, or even no money down. *p. 61*

> Example: If you put $5,000 down on a $100,000 house, and the value of the house goes up 5% after one year, you have gained $5,000 on an investment of $5,000, for a 100% return.

❑ **Borrow to invest** and **pay cash for personal purchases**. Most people do the exact opposite.

❑ Make the interest on a **personal loan tax-deductible** by cashing other investments to pay off the loan, and then borrowing the same amount back to invest in something else. *p. 143*

> Example: Valerie has a $10,000 car loan charging 12% interest, and $5,000 of Canada Savings Bonds earning 8%. She cashes the CSBs and applies the $5,000 against the car loan. Then she borrows $5,000 at 10% interest to invest in a balanced mutual fund, and ends up with the same net worth and total debt payments as before. But now, she has extra tax deductions because the $500 ($5,000 x 10%) of interest expense for borrowing to invest is deductible.

❑ Consider leveraging some **equity in your home**.

- For many, most of their net worth is in real estate (their home), which is poor diversification, and for most areas won't give the great returns of the past.

DO'S AND DON'TS

❑ Do **learn more**. Monitor your investments. Keep up to date on consumer, investment, and tax-reduction opportunities. Read financial books, magazines, newspapers, and check out the internet. Attend free financial planning seminars. *p. 138*

> Example: Anita is 25 years from retirement and starts a pay-yourself-first plan for $4,000 a year. She averages 10% growth a year. If she invests 10 hours a year to learn how to save an extra $1,000 a year, and how to increase her investment returns by only 2%, she will end up with an extra $270,000 at retirement. This works out to over **$1,000 an hour.**

❑ Do **deal with a good, trusted financial advisor**, who will help you achieve *your* unique financial goals. Take advantage of their expertise to keep up to date on new opportunities to invest effectively and reduce taxes. *p. 39*

- Get several referrals from friends, interview them, and choose the one who you are comfortable with and can offer the best service.

❑ Do **buy a home** (when the market and/or interest rates are low). Any rise in the value of your home is tax-free when you sell. *p. 60*

- Don't view a mortgage negatively as a mountainous debt. A mortgage is a highly-leveraged, forced savings plan into what has historically been one of the best long-term investments available: real estate.

❑ Do invest for your **children's education.** *p. 150*

- Get a **20% government grant** on the first $2,000 of annual contributions to an **RESP** (Registered Education Savings Plan). Growth is tax-deferred, and, if used for education, taxed in the child's name when withdrawn to pay little, if any, tax. RESP contributions are limited to $4,000 per year, to a lifetime limit of $42,000 per beneficiary.

If the child doesn't go to school, up to $50,000 of growth can be transferred to your RRSP, or recovered after paying a 20% penalty on top of your tax rate. See your advisor about details on eligibility for the grant, carrying forward unused grant room, and naming multiple beneficiaries. *p. 152*

- The **Child Tax Benefit** can be invested 'In Trust For' the child into any type of investment. The money belongs to the child and faces little, if any, taxation. *p. 150*

- You can invest any amount in **equity mutual funds** 'In Trust For' a child and get most of the benefits of RESPs without any risk of losing the growth. You must pay tax on any interest and dividend income, but most of the growth will be a capital gain in the child's name, and thus face little, if any, tax. See your advisor to set up the informal trust properly. *p. 151*

❑ **Don't ignore your pension** until retirement. Be aware of your options today, and take advantage of them. *p. 101*

❑ Do take advantage of **stock option plans**, where the company adds a portion of whatever stock you buy, if the company is solid.

❑ Do regularly check what government **grants and incentive programs** are available, if you have a business. *p. 157*

> Example: Mario needed an office assistant. Being aware of the government's training program, he received an $8,000 grant to hire and train the new employee.

❑ Do **name a beneficiary** for all investments, particularly RRSPs. If you name your spouse or your minor child as the beneficiary of the RRSP, it is transferred to them tax-free. Otherwise it is taxed at death as income, and the heir loses as much as 50% to income taxes. *p. 119*

❑ Do keep **excess cash reserves** (more than 3 months' expenses) in a money market fund instead of a bank account to earn an extra 2% – 5% a year. *p. 130*

> Example: Tanya moved $5,000 from a bank account to a money market fund and earns an extra 3%, or $150 a year.

❑ Do **keep it simple**. Never invest in anything you do not understand. If you are not comfortable with something, either learn enough to become comfortable, or stay away.

❑ Do **make a will** and keep it up to date. Everyone should have a will to prevent unnecessary expense and delay in settling the estate. *p. 48*

"Help a Friend"

If you found this book valuable, think of the others you know who could also benefit from lowering their expenses and increasing their investment returns. Why not *"Help a Friend"* by referring them to *Financial Freedom Without Sacrifice*? Or, you could give them a copy of their own.

The Perfect Gift

Financial Freedom Without Sacrifice makes the perfect gift for birthdays, Christmas, graduations, or anytime. Entertaining and easy to understand, it is an inexpensive, yet thoughtful gift that is *guaranteed* to be appreciated — or your money back.

Financial Workshops

Financial Success Strategies offers a variety of employer-sponsored and public workshops. Entertaining and valuable, these workshops are an effective way to enhance employee compensation and satisfaction, leading to increased commitment in the workplace. Write for details, or call (519) 663-2252.

Fund-Raising Opportunity

Does your charity, church, or association need to raise funds? Bought at a significant discount, *Financial Freedom Without Sacrifice* is a unique fund-raising product that everyone can benefit from. Write for details, or call (519) 663-2252 to see how Financial Success Strategies can help promote your non-profit campaign.

Financial Freedom Without Sacrifice
Information and Order Form

Valuable, entertaining, and guaranteed to benefit the reader, *Financial Freedom Without Sacrifice* is the perfect gift or promotional item.

❑ Yes, please rush me _____ copies of *Financial Freedom Without Sacrifice* at $14.99 each, including all taxes and shipping. I have enclosed a cheque payable to Financial Success Strategies Inc. for the amount of $_____ (Cdn).

Full Name: _____

Address: _____

City: _____   Province: _____

Postal Code: _____   Phone: _____

More Information

❑ Yes, send details about your financial workshops.

❑ Yes, send details about the fund-raising opportunity.

Feedback Please

Comments or suggestions to improve this book.

_____

_____

_____

Significant discounts (minimum 50% off) are available for orders of 10 books or more. Volume prices range from $7.50 to $6.50, depending on quantity. Write for more details, or call (519) 663-2252.

Financial Success Strategies Inc.
42 Fawn Court, London
Ontario, Canada, N5X 3X3

Please allow four to six weeks for delivery.